Traffic of Life

Characteristics of Effective Leadership

Rick Winters
Omar Reid
Alisa Manning Peppers

Complete Personal Resurrection Seminars

Traffic of Life

Characteristics of Effective Leadership

By Winters, Reid, and Peppers

Copyright 2003 by Winters, Reid and Peppers

First Edition

Bowker's, Books In Print

ISBN 0-9741019-0-7

Printed in the United States of America

Cover Design by Al DeSouza, My Digital Graphics

Printed on acid-free paper

Published by:
Complete Personal Resurrection Seminars, Houston, TX

Table of Contents

Acknowledgments

Thanks to my loving wife Corliss and son Brandon for their outstanding support throughout the completion of this book. Thanks to my family and friends for always encouraging me to pursue my dreams. In addition, I thank Gwen, Val, John and Uncle Troy for their inspiring suggestions. Also, I thank my Lord and savior Jesus Christ for giving me strength and providing me the road map and vision to complete this project.

Rick Winters

Thanks to my wonderful wife Janice who has been by my side throughout this entire process. Without her support, all that I accomplish would not be possible. Thanks to my daughter Briana who continues to motivate me to move mountains. You are the best daughter a dad could have. Thanks to my parents for inspiring me to get an education. Finally I thank all my family and friends who make my life complete.

Omar Reid

It goes without saying that I have been through the traffic of life. Through dead-ends, detours, and wrong turns, my husband, Reggie Peppers, has been right there with the road map. He has been my supporter and motivator. I thank my daughter Morgan for making me feel that I can do anything that I want to do. I thank the strongest woman I know, my mother, for making me the woman that I am today. I also want to thank my family and all of my friends who said, "You can do it."

Alisa Manning Peppers

We would like to thank Tia Shabazz and Cherryl Floyd-Miller for all of their hard work and patience. We would like to thank Mack E. Smith for his direction and leadership. Thank you all for making this book happen.

CPR Seminars

TRAFFIC INTRODUCTION

Imagine you are a young teenager, and you dream of owning your own car. You envision all the things you might do to fix it up, to make it yours. During your senior year in high school, you finally get that car—a '78 Granada painted gray with rusted spots.

This Granada is not your dream car. It does not have the regal look of a Mercedes, the speed of a Ford Mustang, nor the comfort of a Lexus. It is, however, capable of transporting you from one point to another, depending on the amount of gas that you can afford.

The Granada requires a bit of personal attention: You have to constantly add water, transmission fluid, and fuel injector cleaner to reduce the backfiring. After a thorough detailing and a good oil change, though, it looks and runs as good as new.

You are delighted the first day you drive to school alongside Lexuses, Mercedes, and Jaguars. In your heart, you believe your '78 Granada is capable of doing all the things those luxury and sports cars can do; it certainly revs and idles like all the rest. In the vast horde of cars, your Granada has everything it needs to let you ride as smoothly as possible. With continued upkeep, your car could even help you come out ahead of the pack.

If you want to live your life as a leader–a person whose behavior guides and inspires others–you will be required to drive down the paths of your life in the same way that you navigate a highway. You will have to map out routes and decide whether to turn left or right; look over your shoulder when switching lanes; and become more alert in times of inclement weather. The more experience you have, the more confident you become at making crucial decisions on the road.

It is important to be a good driver, one who practices safe driving techniques and has some idea of where he is going before he hits the road. Good drivers are aware of other drivers and distinguish themselves from bad drivers because they obey traffic laws. Bad drivers never follow the rules. They take short cuts, never plan for trips, and almost never communicate in traffic, which can cause accidents.

In the traffic of life, good drivers are also good leaders. More specifically, they create positive, energetic environments; develop other leaders; maintain good health; adapt to obstacles; and embrace the inevitable change that happens daily in a diverse work force. Leaders can affect desired outcomes because they are creative, self-motivated, and willing to go the distance. They are effective planners, good communicators, and they are ready to be responsible drivers.

This book aims to motivate you to act. We want you to be an effective leader—a good driver. We describe the qualities of an effective leader using examples derived from common experiences of everyday driving. In addition this book provides supplemental reading recommendations to further your development. It does not matter if you are a manager at United Parcel Service (UPS) or a worker at Jack in the Box, nor whether you drive a '78 Granada or a current-year Mercedes. We have provided common scenarios from everyday life to help you think about the traffic of your life and how you are currently driving in it. Buckle up. You have an exciting journey ahead of you.

CHAPTER ONE

Learning the Rules

(Desire)

If you believe it, you can achieve it.

Each day when I walk out of my home and get into my car, I want it to start. I complete my morning routine almost the same way daily. One Friday morning, before I turned the key, I felt confident that my car would start. I needed to be at work early so I could complete some work from the previous day. I had an important meeting with a new client, and I wanted everything to go well.

Since it was cold, I knew that I had better let the car warm up. I was running about ten minutes early and would have extra time if I just kept on schedule. As I opened the garage door, I was already planning which task I would complete as soon as I walked into the office. I got in the car and turned the key. Much to my dismay, I heard a sound that let me know something was wrong with the car. *Dead battery*, I thought. I had been in such a hurry the night before that I had left the lights on all night. I had been on a time-sensitive mission and would be delayed by a car problem.

I had two choices in this situation: I could continue to try to accomplish my task or I could let this obstacle stop me. I wanted to complete my task. Would I do it? Would I give in and let a dead battery stop me?

There are legitimate reasons we often give ourselves for not completing all the things we want to accomplish — time constraints, physical limitations, uncooperative behavior of others ... the list goes on. However, in any given situation where you face an obstacle, you are the leader. You can decide how you are going to navigate your way over, around, or through an obstacle. So, the question always becomes: *What do you desire to do?*

Desire is the first fundamental principle of leadership. You have to want to get where you need to go. As a leader, your level of desire can make the difference between survival, stability and success. Desire is the one leadership characteristic that stands out from the rest. Every successful leader has it. Even when it seems he or she is at a point of peril, it is not talent that saves a leader. It is not luck, money, timing, or the good deeds of others. It is the sheer desire one has to change a current situation. Great walls have been erected, tall buildings have been built, and man has even walked on the moon because someone had a desire to accomplish these goals. Desire is fuel, and if you don't have any in your tank you can't possibly move anywhere.

Think for a moment of the fable about the tortoise and the hare. It is a story of desire. With a heavy outer shell and thick, stumpy limbs, the turtle is equipped to move slower. The rabbit, a swift hopper, is able to cover a greater distance in a shorter time. They decide to race, and it seems inevitable that the rabbit will win. The rabbit is so confident, in fact, that he decides to take a nap. There's no way the turtle can catch him, right?

What the rabbit didn't count on, though, was the turtle's desire to be steadfast and consistent. Furthermore, he never imagined the turtle could be a strategist, using his desire to fuel himself toward a strong finish. The turtle was focused, and speed did not matter. The rabbit was not focused and, in the end, speed did not matter for him either. The spoils belonged to the one who followed through on his desire.

In the traffic of life, having the turtle's kind of desire — the kind that leaders have — will help you manage the challenges that are unavoidable in your daily life. Some of us seem to conquer challenges with ease. For others, it seems a tougher labor. Often, I have found myself in discussions with colleagues about the age-old question: Are leaders born or raised? I believe the answer is both. Leaders are both born and raised. You can be born with the desire to succeed, or you can learn this desire after you're born.

I am amazed at the number of people who come up with great ideas but lack the desire to act on them. Someone once told me: *If you want to find good ideas, look in a cemetery, because most people die with great ideas without ever acting upon them.* As a planet, we should have the goal of not burying ideas with bodies. And if we could comb those graves and resurrect the good ideas that have been buried there, would we, the living, have the desire to act upon them now? That would depend: Who among us considers himself a leader?

If you are new to leadership — meaning you've only recently begun to consider yourself a leader or you have just received a new title or position that makes others look to you as a leader — you may be feeling that you don't know all the rules. Perhaps you have mastered your desire and you are feeling uneasy about leadership. You may feel that you need a rule book.

When you first learned how to drive, you were probably given a driver's handbook. That handbook contained every rule you needed to pass the driving test. If you were like me you spent much time going over that handbook to prepare for the test. My friends and I quizzed each other to see if we could come up with *the* question that would stump the others, the one that only the questioner could answer. When it was time to take the test, you were confident because you had prepared. Your desire to pass the test motivated you to prepare.

New leaders must prepare themselves. Not having a rule book in hand is an obstacle that is easy to overcome. There are twenty-five leadership characteristics described in this book. Begin there. Learn these characteristics and make them part of your life. It won't be easy. Change never is. If you have the desire, though, it will be possible.

One of the first things you should do once you know you have the desire to reach a goal is to write it down. Writing down your goals forces you to make a commitment to yourself and automatically makes your goals more than just an oral commitment. A written contract with yourself is more concrete than an oral contract. Get it in writing. This sets the desire mechanism into motion and takes the desire from conceptual to physical.

After you've written your goals, the next thing you should do is tell your friends and family. Sometimes people in your immediate environment can help you stay on course. For example, if you have a desire to lose weight your family may be of assistance when they see you eating something that is not consistent with your desire.

The third thing is something you should be prepared to do when you veer off course. Be ready to jump-start your desire. Sometimes having desire is not enough if your battery is low. Leaders are human and often require a boost to get going again when their desire level needs to be recharged. Call a motivational coach. Listen to inspirational tapes. Meditate. Do whatever it takes to re-energize your desire. Don't let a dead battery stop you.

I started this story by telling you about the day I had to deal with a dead battery. I arrived late to work that day. The meeting started without me, and the client decided to use someone else. However, I did not stop pursuing that client. A few weeks later, I flew to the client's corporate headquarters and made a presentation that landed another contract, much larger than the one I lost earlier. I had a desire to do business with them that could not be diminished by a dead car battery.

What is stopping you from pursuing your dreams or completing your goals? Do you have the desire? Let's start driving and find out.

START

Creating a "mission statement" for your life, a statement of what you value and what you hope to accomplish in your life.

Writing a list of five things you desire most.

Including your friends and family in your hopes and dreams.

Believing leaders can be developed.

Believing you are born to be a winner.

STOP

Having life goals that are not written down.
Giving up on what you desire most at the first sign of failure.

Giving up on your natural talent and accepting a role that will not challenge you.

Listening to people who always say "That won't work."

CHAPTER TWO

Wash Your Car

(Attitude)

"Any fact facing us is not as important as our attitude toward it, for that determines our success or failure."

Norman Vincent Peale

If a friend wanted to ride in the passenger's seat of your car, could he get into the car without removing something–a book, paper, briefcase, or those fast-food bags that you should have thrown away? Is the outside of your car so dirty that someone could easily use a finger to write "Wash Me" in the dust and grime that has collected on the trunk?

If you can answer yes to either of those questions, then you know that your car needs to be cleaned. Perhaps you just haven't had the time. At the moment that your car gets cleaned, though — whether you take it to a car wash or do it yourself in your driveway— something will happen when you get into that clean car. You will deeply inhale. The car will smell better. It will look better. You will feel better sitting inside of it. You will wear a smile as you promise yourself that you'll never let it get that dirty again, though you know that within weeks—often within days—it will need soap and water again.

In the traffic of life, a clean car fosters your best positive attitude; it can change everything. When your traffic of life car gets dirtied with negative energy—grudges, negative thoughts about others, the heavy misfortunes of others, stress, self-doubt, pessimism and any other self-defeating postures, you need to find a car wash fast. Nobody wants to be around negative energy. Unattended, an inclination toward the negative begins to layer itself and affect everything that you touch.

Sometimes, dirt and grime become so much a part of your everyday drive that no one else wants to be near you either. They fear you will make them dirty ... and you will. Negativity spreads, but the redeeming factor is that it can also be washed away. You, the leader, make a choice about whether you will work to stay cleansed or wallow in dirt. You may find self-serve car washes (mediation, visualization of goals, prayer, a good night's sleep, exercise, etc.) and full-service car washes (family, friends, books, audio tapes, inspirational material, sports, and hobbies) to help you rid yourself of anything that does not help your traffic of life car look and ride at optimum capacity.

On your leadership path, you are not immune to being tainted with negativity. You can't escape it. It's a driving condition. You are human, so it is possible to cross a spot in the highway that muddies your vision and splatters debris all over you. Naysayers and office gossips may make you doubt yourself. Supporters may turn their backs on you. Sheer fatigue may make you give less than your best effort to your goals. Your challenge as a leader is to find ways to renew yourself in the midst of doubt. Use negativity as an opportunity to wash your car.

A positive outlook changes the way you drive through life. You'll make different decisions. You move through your day more efficiently. Your stress levels are lower. You feel good about yourself and the people around you. As a leader, you are in a position to effect change in many lives. The life you affect most, though, is your own. Do it with a positive attitude. Do it with a clean car.

START

Smiling. It's a positive attitude adjuster.

Building your self-esteem by focusing on what you can control, not what you cannot.

Choosing to be positive in everything you say. Think about each response. Attitude is a choice.

Relaxing and enjoying your life by doing things "you" enjoy.

Remember that success is having balance in your life. Don't let one area of your life destroy all the other good things.

STOP

Frowning. It's a negative attitude adjuster.

Focusing on others and letting them dictate your mood.

Trying to do it all or be it all. Take it one day at a time.

CHAPTER THREE

Use a Map

(Goals)

"Plan to win, prepare to win, and expect to win."

Zig Ziglar

You've got a clean car, and you have someplace to go. Now you need to determine how you will get there. What route will you take? A scenic route that lets you see major attractions? The quickest route that places you at your destination at a designated time? The least expensive route, minus toll booths and mountain inclines that require more gas? You need a map, a visual representation of all the roads you could possibly take to get to where you're going.

Maps have the delightful function of allowing you to see what lies ahead. You can see where the rivers and lakes lie; how far apart the cities are; where railroads cross; or how far the highways extend north, south, east and west. While you won't be able to account for everything you might encounter—you won't see construction zones or detours nor the areas where traffic slows during rush hour or because there's been an accident—you are able to get a clear picture of your path. You can see *how to get there* (your destination) *from here* (your current place).

Mapping your life goals serves the same kind of function. You envision what is possible by writing it down. A written plan is tangible and makes you accountable to yourself for the goals you've set. You are able to mark milestones and inspire yourself to keep moving forward.

Have you ever planned a dream vacation and discussed all the things you wanted to do when you arrived at your dream location? But when you returned home, you wished you had written down beforehand all the things you really wanted to accomplish while on that dream vacation?

Ronnie, a mechanical engineer, did. He planned a family trip to California with his wife and son. A month prior to the trip, he wrote down all of the activities he wanted to do. He made a list of all the things he needed to take to ensure those activities were accomplished. In addition, he had a map and identified specific rest locations along the way. He knew the distance of the trip and even tracked the weather. Ronnie and his family had a memorable trip and accomplished most of the things he'd written down. He had *planned* the trip, and it made all the difference in the quality of his family's vacation.

Ronnie started his adventure to California as a dream vacation, but it materialized as more than a dream, simply because he wrote it down.

Leaders often write down their goals. They create a map of their journey to guide them and ensure they don't get lost. Imagine Ronnie taking a trip to California from Texas with no map to use as a guide. The chances are pretty high that he would have gotten lost and, worse, that he might never have seen the attractions that he had planned to see.

In your traffic of life car, you might have to map your journey for the next three to five years. *Where is it that you want to be at that time?* Writing it down helps you understand what it will take for you to reach your destination. It moves you to get there. The reason this approach works for most leaders is simple: If you can see it, then it can happen. The challenges that you may encounter along the way–heavy traffic on the road, time required to eat, a flat tire, construction, engine trouble–won't matter because you've already mapped your way. And if you already have a map, it's easy to re-route yourself in the event that something prevents you from moving ahead.

Effective leaders "plan to win, prepare to win and expect to win." Leaders must be excellent planners, goal-setters, and developers. Having a mission statement and goals for your team is essential for your success. You cannot lead a group of people if you have no sense of direction. Neither you nor your team will get anywhere. The direction you need often doesn't become clear for you until you write it down. If your goal is to achieve your cost plan for the year, for example, it is wise to know the cost goal for each month and write it down. This helps you determine whether you're on the right path. Make sure you document the status of last year's results and you will have clearly projected the path to your goal. When you don't, you risk losing your way and, eventually, failing to achieve the goal.

Sometimes the map you create for your drive will be a rough representation of your journey. It may be hand-drawn with rudimentary symbols. It still serves the purpose of getting you to a destination. Other times, you will have more sophisticated tools at your disposal to plot your trip. For example, some of the new model cars are equipped with mapping technology, an electronic device that provides you with directions at the touch of a button. Some mapping technology has the capability to let you communicate with a live person to direct you to your desired location. You simply need the coordinates and an address, which functions somewhat like a mission statement. The address, your mission, says exactly where you need to go.

As a leader, having those initial coordinates–a mission statement–helps you at times when you lose your way. You can always refer back to a mission statement. In fact, review it regularly to ensure you are not distracted by some of the beautiful attractions that you encounter along the way. Place your mission statement in a place where you can look at it often to remind you of where you're going.

You should also have a different map –at home, at work, at church or any other place where you should be consciously aware of your goals for each journey that you're on. At church, your religious text (Bible, Torah, Koran) are your maps. At work, corporate managers may provide organizational maps for you. Hopefully, you and your supervisor have made some employee development goals for your career. There is something completely affirming about making the same kind of map for your family. It says you plan to get somewhere together, that you intend to last as a unit into infinity. Successful families have created strong, detailed maps and are already driving toward bright futures.

There are several maps leaders can use to make sure they are going in the right direction. For example, the effective use of a daily planner or Palm Pilot can serve as a guide for the things you want to accomplish on a daily, monthly, and yearly basis. Leaders should keep diaries of events that occur throughout the course of a year and communicate goals to their teams. *What goals have you identified for your team at work? Can each team member repeat the same goals you have identified? Is your map in sync with your team's map?* It's very important that each member on the team understand the goals you are trying to achieve and their role in helping the team to achieve those goals.

As a leader, you must make sure goals are measurable, attainable, and desirable. The results of the goals you want to achieve should be posted for all team members to see. When your team is on the same page, mistakes are reduced, accidents don't simply happen, and goals are achieved. To return to the example of the dream vacation, if Ronnie planned that dream vacation and his brother was going to follow him on the trip, he should outline the trip and ensure his brother has the same map he does. As the leader in that situation, Ronnie should provide clear direction for his team. Has someone ever given you bad directions and you got lost following them? How did you feel? Did you trust that person's directions again?

As a leader, it should be difficult to imagine being without a map to direct your team. When you have a project to complete and it requires input from several departments, it's imperative that meetings are held regularly to ensure everyone understands the plan. Communicate your goals to the entire team. In most cases, when leaders fail, it's because the team has different objectives than the leader.

It is also important to remember that maps change. Each year, new streets are added, new landmarks are built, and highways are extended. Maps need to be the most current representation of the roads you may travel in order to get you accurately to a destination. Otherwise, you may be driving and looking for a street that is no longer there. Goals–the maps for your life–also become outdated. Don't be afraid to change them. As the environment in which you work and live evolves, so should your goals. You can't safely count on getting somewhere if you're working with an obsolete map.

Having a successful game plan is essential to your success as a leader. Your desire and passion to achieve these goals must move your people to achieve the same goals, too. Having a clearly outlined map helps you and your team to reach a destination. Without it, you are simply driving aimlessly without a tangible place to go.

START

Using a Palm Pilot® or daily planner to write down your goals each day.

Training team members to achieve goals.

Establishing goals for your family.

Reviewing your goals daily.

STOP

Keeping the goals from team members.

Setting unrealistic goals.

Setting goals and not reviewing results regularly.

CHAPTER FOUR

Your Service Light is On

(Health/Energy)

"Health is not valued till sickness comes."

Dr. Thomas Fuller

When you first start your car in the morning, the first thing you should see is the vehicle indicators that light up when your car is started. Those lights tell you how much gas you have, what the oil level is, whether it's time for water, or to check the engine after a certain amount of mileage. The indicators tell you how well the body of your car is working; they tell you if something needs attention. What if your service light is on? What should you do? Sit and stare at the light hoping it will go away? Or do you react immediately and take it to a dealer or mechanic for service? In many cases, you might ignore the service light because you believe you have sufficient time to correct the problem before something irreparable goes wrong.

In the traffic of life, the service light indicator might be telling you that you need to take care of yourself. Your body eventually reacts in some way to tell you what it needs. If you find yourself with consistent migraine headaches, stomach pains, sore joints, and back pains that have not been diagnosed, it may be your body's service indicator. You shouldn't ignore it or hope that you have plenty of time to keep going before something irreparable happens. Usually, if you keep putting it off, it is probable you will wait until your body is not able to function any more. If your health reaches this point of desperation, the liability is yours.

What stops you from going in for maintenance? A simple check-up? Some leaders use the excuse that they have to keep going. Despite the blinking lights inside the car telling them that they need to head to a physician for an exam or take a moment of rest to regenerate energy, they are more concerned that they have somewhere to go and must get there.

Perhaps the reason is cost. Going to get a check-up costs money that you've convinced yourself you simply don't have. In the long-term, you can't afford *not* to go. Over time, an ignored health condition becomes more costly. You will pay far more money for aggravated health issues than you would for the simple things that you ignore. Headaches can become tumors; stomach pains can become gastrointestinal disease, back pain can become paralysis. You must deal with your indicators now, or you will deal with them later when the stakes are much higher.

Let's look at another key dash indicator: the temperature gauge, which tells you whether your radiator is working properly. That gauge can go to two extremes, hot or cold, and will usually do so before you begin to hear overheating sounds coming from beneath the hood. By the time the car is overheated, it is hissing, choking off, blowing smoke and steam, moving slower, and blurring your vision. The stress of continuing to drive under these conditions eventually shuts your car down. The car itself forces you to pull over, turn off the engine and rest.

In the traffic of life, an inordinate amount of stress can make you overheat in the same manner. Careers and goals can place leaders under a lot of pressure and trigger the onset of health problems if they don't take preventive measures. Like a radiator, your body can handle only so much heat before it explodes and will not run anymore. You don't want your body to forcibly shut down or to require you to park in order to let your engine cool off. How many vehicles can drive continuously without the driver taking an opportunity to pull over and cool off? The same can be said in life. It becomes imperative that we take the time to park our cars and get enough rest. You want to choose your moments of rest. Make them planned times for maintenance not emergency exits from the highway.

If there is something physically wrong, it is possible that there won't necessarily be some warning light or steam from a radiator to warn you. Sometimes you can get from point A to point

B and never see that something is internally wrong. The rotors may be bad or the alternator may be going out. In those situations, preventive care for your car helps keep it in top running condition.

In the traffic of life, leaders must make sure that they are not merely healthy, but fit. If you take a physical exam that shows no high blood pressure, heart complications, diabetes, cancer, or anything else that deteriorates your body, then you are healthy. However, if you find yourself struggling to make it up one flight of stairs, you are not fit. You are in survivor mode. Leaders don't settle for just being healthy. In his book "Over the Top," Zig Ziglar says leaders can make a difference in this world by moving from survivor mode to stability and from stability to significance. Leaders want to do more than just survive. Being fit–stable and significant–gives you more energy, drive, ideas, and more time to live a quality life.

Besides the fact that effective leaders must be able to crank their cars immediately under any given circumstance, why is physical fitness so important? Why must you keep your battery charged? Or gas in your fuel tank? When you lead a group of people, most of those people feed off of your energy. They depend on that energy to be the example for their own lives, to tow them along when their energies are low. If you, the leader, don't have enough gas to make it all the way to your destination, how can you expect to lead and inspire others? Energy allows you to get through the day, week, month, and year. Energy is the fuel for everyday leadership. Here's a story about a leader who didn't understand the importance of not running out of gas:

I remember the time I had a very important meeting, and I noticed my gas light was on. I failed to get gas the previous night because I was tired and did not feel like stopping. The weather was cold, and there was a slight rain coming down. I just wanted to make it home and deal with getting gas tomorrow.

I rolled out of bed twenty minutes later than planned and if I had stopped to get gas I would have been late for my meeting. I decided I would try to make it with the amount of gas I had. As I was speeding down the highway, the gas light came on again, alerting me that it was time to refuel. A sign ahead informed me that my exit was only two miles away, and I had another eight miles to my destination.

I exited the freeway and approached the light at the intersection. As I sat at the red light, I hoped I would see a gas station nearby. The light turned green and I started to enter the intersection. I heard my car make a sputtering sound. I pushed the gas again and the same sputtering sound came out. My biggest fear had become real: I was out of gas in the middle of an intersection.

I had a blank look on my face as I wondered, "How could this happen to me?" I had stopped traffic. Everybody glared at me as they passed me in the intersection. Their evil stares seemed to be saying, "What are you, an idiot or something? How could you not know you needed gas? Thanks a lot, smart guy, for delaying my day and making me late for work!"

The street noise seemed louder than usual as I got out of my car and started to walk to the nearest gas station.

In the traffic of life, there are many ways to refuel. Just as gas stations are located throughout a city, gymnasiums, parks, and nutritional stores are there for you to refill your body with energy. Exercise and proper nutrition provide the necessary energy to keep your tank full. Sometimes, we ignore the need to exercise in order to fuel our bodies using the excuse of being too tired. Well, guess what? Your traffic of life car will never move if you are too tired to go get gas. What if you never go to the gas station and continually put it off for another day—a day that never comes. How would your car move?

As a leader, are you driving with your gas light or other service indicators on? How do you know when you are out of gas? You know when you have poor production at work, poor relationships, are not exercising, listening, or you find you are overeating and lack creativity. Each of these challenges is a fuel light indicator telling you to refuel.

As you arrive at a filling station to refuel, you have other choices to make. What kind of fuel should you pump into your tank? The least expensive? Premium Octane? Unleaded Plus? Regular Unleaded? The decision you make can also determine the performance level for your car. You may not want to put Premium Unleaded in your tank because you think the cost is too high. Unleaded Plus will still get your engine humming but does not give you the same performance as Premium Unleaded. Regular Unleaded is the most economical. The decision rests squarely on how you want your car to run.

You make the same choices about what type of fuel to put in your body. You can use the Premium Unleaded, which is a complete exercise program and proper nutrition. Unleaded Plus consists of sporadic exercise and moderate diet. Regular Unleaded which is a quick-fix diet plan and minimal exercise. Your choice determines how effectively you run in the race of life. Sometimes the cost difference between Unleaded and Premium is significant, and sometimes the difference is not immediately noticeable at all. However, when you need that something extra to overcome those daily obstacles and stresses, it makes a difference what type of gas you put in your tank that day.

What can bad gas do to an engine? It can make your car

smoke or backfire. A diet that is more harmful to your health than good can make your body backfire. Living a healthy life will give you the energy needed to face your daily challenges and accomplish your goals.

Energy is like a forest fire: It can start off small with one person but can spread to many. You don't want to spread low energy to the people who are led and influenced by you. Energize yourself by living a healthy lifestyle and following an exercise program. Pay attention to your body when your indicator lights are flashing. Make sure that you are not forced by an unexpected breakdown to the side of the road.

START

Scheduling an exercise program.

Taking vitamins daily.

Eating a well-balanced diet.

Eating breakfast every morning.

Reading health magazines.

Drinking more water.

Getting annual physicals

Getting enough rest.

STOP

Smoking and excessive drinking.

Eating large meals late at night.

Ignoring the importance of going to the doctor.

Using quick-fix diets.

CHAPTER FIVE

Windshield Wipers

(Vision)

"Cherish your visions and your dreams as they are the children of your soul; the blueprints of your ultimate achievements."

Napoleon Hill

On the road, storms can be the most likely obstacles to prevent you from reaching your destination. Sometimes, it is simply not safe to keep going. At other times, a storm is a test of your willingness to see beyond your immediate line of sight. Here is a story from a woman whose family weathered a storm to find vision:

One weekend, we were traveling to a family reunion during a rainstorm. This was going to be one of our biggest reunions. We convinced everyone in the family to make the road trip. There were three or four cars coming from the Houston area, all leaving at different times and from different places. The plan was to meet at our grandmother's house by 2:00 p.m. As we traveled early that morning, the rain began coming down lightly. My husband put the windshield wipers on so that he could see better.

As we got further down the highway, the rain grew heavier. My husband adjusted the wipers to help with visibility. The sky darkened, and we began to worry. He put the wipers on high and we slowed down. Visibility was so bad that we couldn't see the car ahead of us. We thought about pulling over but decided to go forward anyway.

Slowly, we drove through the storm as the rain poured. The car was quiet as we both strained to see the road and wondered if the rain would ever end. We turned off the radio and focused on the road ahead. After several miles, the rain started to let up. My husband adjusted the wipers. Suddenly, the rain was gone. Just like that, we could see clearly the clouds behind us.

We looked at each other and laughed. We had just gone

though a pocket of rain that only lasted a few miles, although we had no way of knowing that it would be so short. If we hadn't had our windshield wipers to help us see, we would have stopped and sat in the middle of the storm. We would have never guessed that we would drive right through it in such a short period of time.

Of course, the major lesson to be learned from this story is that you can make it through a storm. Even when your vision is blurred, you can stay on your path and move safely toward your destination. The second thing to remember is that the distance from the most turbulent moment of a storm to a clearer, more peaceful time may be as short as five minutes. Storms don't last forever.

In the traffic of life, leaders need clear vision, even when in the midst of a storm. There is no easy way to maneuver through the storms of your life. It is hard to drive when there is a torrential downpour blurring your vision and slowing you down. It's hard to see, you become tense, and other drivers become a concern. Even if you have the best map for your trip, certain unforeseen hazards, like heavy rain, can slow down your pace. Storms significantly slow traffic. You must use greater caution and watch for sudden stops by other vehicles. You have two important tools to navigate your way through these moments: focus and windshield wipers.

What serves as a leader's windshield wipers in a storm? On a very basic level, it's physical. Those individuals a leader surrounds himself with keep him on course during a storm. They encourage him to keep going. In the absence of those people, it can be something else that a leader connects with physically that motivates him to keep going. It may be inspirational books, a quote posted on the wall, or a business or yoga course that continually reinforces his ability to visualize goals.

Wipers can also be internal, or spiritual. Perhaps it's a strong conviction or religious belief that motivates you to do what seems impossible. Or maybe it's an internal dialogue you have with yourself to keep going when the task before you seems daunting.

Whatever brings you that clarity in the traffic of life is something you must be able to tap into right away. Good leaders use their windshield wipers as soon as their vision becomes impaired. They don't try to drive ahead without clear sight. This is dangerous. It can lead to tragic business or personal accidents.

Most windshield wipers have settings for different speed levels. During a light mist, level one on the wiper dial is sufficient. You can almost make it without your wipers, but it's easier to move forward if you use them. Here is a light-mist situation you might encounter on a job: Suppose you are a supervisor and must tell your employee that she was not selected for a promotion that she wanted. Instead, she will become the lead worker on your team.

There is potential for a storm here because the employee is not going to get what she wanted. What makes it a light-mist situation, though—one in which you might have to present the benefits of being a lead worker and ask her to invest in your decision—is that she is not being fired. The new tasks that you ask her to take on will give her more responsibility and move her "up" in some ways, but it is not the promotion that she wanted. You could very well just deliver your decision and ask her to take it or leave it. You are the boss and your obligation to her is to deliver your decision. You could easily do only that and move forward through this light-mist situation. However, preparing yourself to give her a presentation of your decision, one that shows her the possibilities of a new career path, allows her to feel her value on your team. You are not merely delivering information; you are communicating with a person you value. When you go the extra step to communicate with her, you turn your light-mist wipers on and give yourself better vision.

Other situations in the traffic of life will require more than light-mist wipers. On rainy days, level one on the wipers won't work; you will need level two. Maybe the storm you're in is a financial or a family storm. You will need more than just your own vision or someone else's opinion. You might need professional assistance, or you might need to involve everyone in your family to see a solution clearly.

Then there are the highest level wiper adjustments that you use during thunderstorms. This wiper level gives you the kind of vision you might need during personal tragedy, like the loss of a loved one or job. It takes the fast motion of high-powered wipers to help you see even the smallest distance in front of you. At times, especially during personal tragedy, this highest level on your wipers is not enough to help you see. Wipers are designed to only do so much. The storm is so powerful (and your vision is so cloudy) that forging ahead will place you in more jeopardy. You can't see the cars around you, the road, or anything ahead of you. If that is the case, it's better to stop and wait for the storm to pass. Don't take the risk of doing anything that you feel is life-threatening. Pull over to the side of the road and take care of yourself.

It is not always easy to know whether to keep going through a storm or to stop. You must weigh the factors and determine what is both safe and effective. There will be instances when people will tell you to slow down, stop, or turn back. You shouldn't. As long as you have focus, you can continue toward your goal even if you are nervous and a little cautious about what lies ahead. As a leader, you must determine the best course of action that is healthy for you and helps you achieve your goal. Think of the woman and her husband on their way from Houston to that family reunion:

There were several times when I thought about telling my husband to stop, but I knew he wanted to arrive as close to 2:00 p.m. as he could and would make adjustments as we went along. We made it to the reunion by 2:00. The other cars coming from Houston didn't. When they arrived, they asked us if we ran into that awful storm. We said it wasn't a storm, just a few miles of bad rain. They'd all pulled over and waited for hours as the rain hovered over those few miles of highway.

The storms in our lives don't last forever and can be overcome if we stay focused on the road. An effective leader is prepared to see his way through a storm. With a laser-like focus, he keeps his vision clear and is always prepared to move steadfast with clarity toward his goal. A storm is his opportunity to size up what lies ahead–an insurmountable rush of rain, wind, thunder, and lightening, or a pocket of rain that he can leave behind after only a few miles.

START

By creating a mission statement for your life, corporation, or organization.

Believing that storms don't last forever.

Having faith in yourself to obtain your goals.

Developing action steps to accomplish your long-term goals

Writing down your current position on a map and drawing a road on paper of where you want to go. Include possible challenges along the way.

STOP

Believing that you can't achieve your dreams.

Moving forward without clear goals.

Letting your doubts or others deter you from success.

Dealing only with the present.

CHAPTER SIX

Construction

(Determination)

"The road to success is always under construction."

Jim Miller

As demonstrated in the following story, dealing with construction on the road can be a huge undertaking, especially if you have a specific place to go and a designated time to get there. It was another hot summer day, around ninety-five degrees and traffic was at its normal standstill with the usual freeway road rage beginning to flare up. My goal was to leave the office by five o'clock and make it home in time to see Sports Center. As I drove along the freeway, and I noticed a sign which read, "Construction ahead five miles." I drove a little farther and the next sign indicated the left lane would be closed for construction. I was amazed. It was rush hour and construction was still in progress on the most-traveled freeway in Houston, Texas. I could not ever recall driving from one location to another in Houston and not observing some form of construction in progress. I became frustrated and wondered when the madness was ever going to end.

I exited the freeway and tried the feeder road but, to my surprise, I was greeted by another orange sign: "Construction ahead. Right lane closed." The time was now five-thirty. I was frustrated at not making any progress toward home, and I began to doubt I would make it in time. Each time I thought I had discovered a successful route to get home, I ran into some form of construction or traffic that slowed me down again. Finally, I remembered a back road that would get me to the Beltway Expressway and, hopefully, home in time. Miraculously, after several failed attempts to beat the traffic and construction, I finally discovered one that did not impede my progress.

Road construction in the traffic of life represents all the challenges you face in life when pursuing your dreams. It is all the road signs and detours that can slow you down. If you are determined, though, if you believe in your destiny enough to find alternative routes, you will get there. Driving through construction sets a much higher standard for you and forces you to use your skills to stay on course. Your goal is not only to get where you're going but also to move efficiently.

Often, the signs on the road are warning signals to help you redirect yourself so that you stay on the path toward your goals. Signs give you options to find an alternate path, one that may not necessarily be what you planned but delivers you to your intended destination anyway. You are always given signs of what challenges lie ahead–that last notice before the lights are turned off, a disturbing phone call from a bill collector, your child's failing report card, or a rejection letter for the job you coveted. These signs tell you that you must face the rigors of construction ahead. They are not stop signs; they are warning signs. So, the news they often bring is not an indication that something is impossible. They are merely helpful hints at what you must do differently to meet your goal. A leader uses a construction sign as a golden opportunity to channel some new direction for himself.

Construction zones are also districts of slow-moving traffic. In most cases, construction signs caution you to reduce your speed because the roads are being repaired. It is much safer for both drivers and construction workers to move at a slower pace. It gives you more reaction time for sudden shifts in the highway, or new traffic patterns caused by bright orange barriers, or newly laid asphalt that does not yet have divider lines. As a result, traffic often comes to a standstill. If you have not been fortunate to find an alternative route, you may feel like you'll never get out of your traffic rut.

Within your traffic of life construction zones (job conflicts, marital strife, financial hardship), you may also feel as if you have come to a complete standstill. Your challenges seem long-term and never-ending. It is at those times that you must either have the patience to drive slowly through the construction or find a quicker, less congested route. You must stay determined. Remember the desire that helps you start your car each morning. Remember that you have a plan, a map that will get you to where you need to be. You have a mission statement to keep you focused. Refer to it frequently. Remind yourself that you have someplace to go and find the will to get there.

You may be tempted to quit. Steve Potter says, "The road to success has many tempting parking spots." Leaders are not quitters. They are not people who are willing to quit on their dreams when the road of life gets too bumpy. A determined spirit is never easily defeated. Determination does not give up. "Some succeed because they are destined to; most succeed because they are determined to." (Anatole France) Road construction does not stop you.

So why must there be construction? We need to evolve, to build roads that serve our changing needs. We need to improve, to make roads that are safer and smoother. We need to connect, to build roads that lead to other roads and give us new options for our journeys. Construction provides hope for things that will come in the future. Most drivers know this, in spite of the frustration they feel when dealing with construction. Once the construction is finally complete, the ride on the new road will be smooth and gratifying.

Don't kid yourself into thinking that the construction is done forever, though. If you live in a major city, you know there will be potholes to fix and additional expansion. There will always be construction. Just when one road is repaired, another is damaged. Just when one goal is achieved, another is set. You feel as if you are always chasing a dream.

How else will you prove your determination? Jose Ortega y Gasset says, "Life is a series of collisions with the future; it is not the sum of what we have been, but what we yearn to be." Colliding with the future is really about understanding that the task of determination is never-ending. It's almost cyclical. Once you drive through a construction zone, there will be others on highways that you have not yet traveled. It is up to you to find an alternative route. It is your keen leadership skills that will help you avoid pulling over at the first rest stop and quitting.

START

Setting a goal. Complete it regardless of the circumstances.

Practicing positive self-talk in the car, around the house, while exercising, etc.

Seeking out mentors and advisors.

Researching those who have overcome similar challenges and use their successes as fuel to achieve your goals.

STOP

Trying to avoid failure. Keep persevering.

Giving up. Success may be only inches away.

Practicing self-criticism. Don't be your own worst enemy.

CHAPTER SEVEN

Drive Safe

(Integrity)

"Those who stand for nothing may fall for anything."

Alexander Hamilton

A set of rules governs the road. Highway safety officials have created regulations to moderate the ways that drivers operate their vehicles. There is something more intimate than that set of rules, however, that governs how you behave on the road. It is an internal constitution, so to speak—a code of ethics that determines how you respond in any given situation. In the most ideal situation, it is a value system that is based on integrity, an incorruptible honesty. It is your sense of right and wrong.

How many times have you been stopped at a red light, in a hurry, and thought you could run it because it would get you to your destination sooner? What about exceeding the speed limit in a school zone because you don't see any children? or passing a radar-equipped police unit and checking your speedometer to see if you were going to receive his next ticket? Or parking in a handicapped parking space because you need to "just run in and out" of the store? Are you like this driver?

My wife and I take many of the same routes to our destinations. If I pass one of the radar units before she does, I will call her on the cell phone to let her know where she needs to slow down.

One of the most important characteristics a leader must possess does not come from a book of rules or written manual. It's his integrity, which, if corrupted, can be detrimental to a leader's success. In a leadership position, your integrity must be intact and beyond question. Leaders who lack integrity will not be respected. There is usually a price to pay if your integrity is spoiled. Many contemporary leaders in both business and politics are discovering this the hard way. They have violated the public trust that was invested in them and have felt the strong repercussions that result from that breached trust. Often, the violation of public trust causes damage beyond repair to social, economic, political, and business systems.

There is a saying that a house built on a solid foundation will be much stronger than one built on an uneven foundation. Corporate environments offer solid proof that this axiom is true. For years now, many Fortune 500 companies have listed integrity as a managerial cornerstone. And they mean it. Any person violating a rule of integrity is dismissed. Many workers, otherwise good people who took shortcuts to achieve something, have been released from employment. They were willing to risk their entire futures on a lie, and it has often caught up with them.

This is true not only at the employee level. It creeps into the upper echelons of management. There are companies whose officers use the gray area of legality to make a profit. When tough questions arise, management cannot be found. If we take this as a sign of our times, we have lost our way as a society. Many cover stories in magazines and newspapers often tell of ethics and morality decay in our world. We have abandoned our integrity.

A perfect recent example is Enron, which was the seventh largest company in the United States before its implosion. Enron's employees were considered some of the best and the brightest in their fields. For years, it was considered a Wall Street favorite, especially since the company met or exceeded analysts' expectations quarter after quarter. Life at Enron seemed great.

One day someone began to question some of the company's accounting practices. More investigation led to the discovery of some major accounting irregularities in the reporting of the company's true financial position. In the end, key leading figures for Enron were found to have known all about it, yet they said nothing. As more evidence of tainted integrity, there was indifference from the auditors, an independent organization that had been entrusted to ensure the accuracy of the numbers. The whole system was faulty, a collapsible house built on an uneven foundation. When it all began tumbling down, it was because no one in a leadership position had the integrity to do the right thing. The entire system had been debased.

Where have we tucked away the days when your word was your bond? There was a time when all one had to live by was his word, when actions reflected the value of that word. There is rarely much redemption for lost integrity. It is hard to rebuild trust once it's been lost. This has become an age of thirty-second election commercials for reigning spin doctors. It is becoming increasingly difficult to find someone who says something and means it.

In the traffic of life, you trust everyone on the road with you to follow the rules. More importantly, you trust yourself to do the same. You know that if you are the last person at a four-way stop, you should be the last person to leave the stop. What would happen if everyone decided not to follow the rules? What if there were no law enforcement officers to hold drivers accountable for traffic violations? How many senseless accidents do you think there would be?

One of the most arresting moments in the legal system is the swearing in of the witness. The reason this moment grips you is because of the oath taken prior to testifying. The bailiff asks the person to raise his or her right hand and "swear to tell *the truth, the whole truth, and nothing but the truth.*" Everything else that a witness says after that moment is measured against the promise of the truth. Onlookers are watching for the tiniest hint that the witness might be unreliable or giving false testimony.

Leaders, too, take this oath. They don't do it in such a public manner or with their right hands raised and their left hands on a

Bible. But when they agree to be leaders, when they accept the position of responsibly inspiring people to reach their greatness, they are taking an oath to do it honestly.

In the traffic of life, this means that leaders follow the rules of the road. They proceed along the highway with a working knowledge of the regulations and drive with integrity.

START

Reading your company's policy book and abiding by it.

Living up to the trust of others placed in you.

Being consistent. Your actions speak louder than your words.

Believing you can be successful by following the rules.

STOP

Lying.

Thinking the rules don't apply to you.

Taking shortcuts to get your desired results.

Allowing others to influence a decision you will regret.

CHAPTER EIGHT

Speed Trap

(Decisions)

"Make up your mind to act decidedly and take the consequences. No good is ever done in this world by hesitation. "

Thomas H. Huxley

The act of making up your mind about something is a process filled with possibilities. You weigh the possible outcomes of a situation and choose to move toward the result that you desire. You believe you have made a sound decision, but what if no one agrees with you? See how the following driver made a solid decision and had to stick by it:

I was driving in traffic one day and was stopped at a red light. There were about five cars ahead of me all waiting in anticipation of the light turning green. When the light changed, the first car rolled through, followed by the next car, and then the third and fourth. When I rolled through, the light turned yellow. My first thought was "Do I slow down or speed up?" If I slowed down, I would end up in the middle of the intersection with honking horns telling me to move out of the way. If I sped up, I would be racing to get out of the way of other cars. Either way, I needed to make a decision. I decided to hit the accelerator and make the light. Now the term "make the light" is relative. I was the last car to go through and, of course, I thought I did everything right. However, minutes later, I saw red and blue lights flashing in my rear view mirror. I checked my speed. I was not speeding. I checked my expiration sticker on my windshield. That had not expired. Well, I thought, this guy must need me to pull over so that he can get by. So I pulled over one lane and noticed he did the same. I moved over again and he followed. It was then that I realized that he was pulling me over for "making the light."

"Ma'am is there a reason you ran the light at that intersection?" he asked. This was perfect. I did have a

good reason. He disagreed, and I received a seventy-five dollar fine as an indication of his disapproval.

In the traffic of life, a leader must make–and stand by decisions. When the officer pulled over the driver above and said that she ran the red light, she disagreed. She explained her decision not to yield and stop because that would have put her in the middle of traffic. She explained that she would have placed others, as well as herself, in danger. The officer didn't buy it and gave her a ticket. The driver was so sure she hadn't run a red light that she chose to go to court and defend her decision. She was required to pay the seventy-five dollars, which means the judge didn't agree with her decision either. She was still certain she was right. She stood by that.

Decision-making is a part of our daily lives. Your choices affect you, your team and, ultimately, your success. Because decision-making can involve so many people, it can be one of the toughest challenges for a leader. It is also one of the most important attributes of a successful leader. No plan can progress without a choice being made so that action can take place. Further, decisions are only as firm as a leader's commitment to standing by them. Perhaps your choice as a leader will not be a popular one, and maybe no one will agree with you. There may even be sacrifices you must make as a result of your decisions. If you make them with integrity and honor them with conviction, then you are on a good path.

Decision-making is just as important as planning and goal setting. It is a process. You ask yourself questions like: *Is this going to benefit the company? How will it affect everyone? Once I have made this decision, can I face the consequences?* Sometimes you have only minutes to make an important decision. During that short interval, you may have to take many lives into consideration and weigh the consequences.

Remember the driver at the traffic light? Either choice she made, she would have had to bear the consequences. Should she have stopped in the middle of traffic or gotten out of the way? She made her decision, though it wasn't the best choice for that situation. As the officer informed her, she should have timed the light and made sure it was green. If presented with that situation again, she will undoubtedly make certain that she drives through a light that is green and not yellow, allowing no one to accuse her of running a red light. She is a leader who will learn from her decisions, good or bad. That is how she improves.

Leaders must make decisions. Not everyone is going to agree with them. Therefore, learn from your mistakes and the mistakes of others. You decide.

START

Trusting your judgment.

Being the expert in your field. Learning is the key to being comfortable in making decisions.

Asking for help. We all need mentors.

Learning from your mistakes.

Being decisive and clear with your message.

Reviewing historical data, to review trends of the past.

STOP

Expecting negative outcomes with every decision.

Being tentative. Make a decision.

Avoiding responsibility for your decisions.

Taking credit for all successful decisions. Remember, it's a team effort.

CHAPTER NINE

Horn, Lights and Signals

(Communication)

" It doesn't cost anything to speak to others. "

Rick Winters

A car has all the trappings of communication. The horn, lights, and turn signals are all designed to help you talk to other drivers. So why is it that drivers fail to use these tools when they need them? Countless drivers fail to use proper signals when changing lanes; they don't blow their horns at impending danger; they don't use headlights in inclement weather; and some even drive at dusk with their lights off.

Failure to communicate with other drivers makes conditions ripe for a mishap. Other drivers must be aware of what you are trying to accomplish on the road. It is essential to everyone's survival.

In the same way, leaders must be able to use the right communication tools to convey the goals and desires of an organization and motivate their teams to reach those goals. Communication builds relationships. It establishes an acquaintanceship–a rapport–between you and some other person or group. In traffic, you build relationships with other drivers; in life, you build relationships daily with other people. The way that you communicate determines the nature of the relationship.

The exchange between you and other drivers is not always positive, although it is communication. Suppose you are sitting at a red stoplight with your foot on the brakes. Because your rear brakes are lit, you are communicating with the driver behind you that you have come to a complete stop and he should follow suit, switch lanes or adjust his speed accordingly. He decides to come to a complete stop behind you. Suddenly, the stoplight turns green. Within one second, the driver in the car behind you repeatedly blows his horn. The relationship has immediately become negative. The way the other driver chose to communicate has shaped the nature of your relationship with him.

At home and work, the way that you choose to communicate with others determines the nature of your relationships with them.

People trust you according to the way that your messages come across to them in conversation. More often than not, it is not the information that you deliver (what you say) that matters most. *How* you deliver that information is what determines the progress of your relationship. This is especially true in emotionally-charged situations. What if you have to fire an employee? Or tell a member of your debate team that he did not make the cut to go to a national competition? If you have always spoken in a positive, respectful tone on a regular basis with the person, you have done well in building that relationship. Your task won't be so difficult. However, if it is your habit to condescend to employees, friends, family, and associates, you can be assured that this will be a rocky conversation.

Leadership is about creating an environment that motivates others to want to achieve positive results. You begin to create that environment for yourself and others when you effectively communicate–in such a way that there is no question about your meaning and intent and in a way that respects everyone involved in the dialogue. Everyone knows how it feels when others don't communicate well, so leaders have a special priority to avoid projecting that same experience into someone else's life.

How many times have you become upset when driving because the person in front of you fails to put on his blinkers and then makes a sharp right turn? The next thing you know you are slamming on your brakes and starting to build a really special relationship with that driver ... the one who communicated poorly and began a chain reaction of events.

In the traffic of life, you, the leader, have an opportunity to decide what kind of communicator you will be. It is probably very closely connected to your leadership style. Will you spit commands at those whom you lead? Will you offer suggestions and guide your team members to a designated goal? Will you lead by inspiration and give them motivational words to complete their tasks? Words are extremely powerful tools and can make your connections to others very relaxed or very strained.

One major shortcoming of some leaders is the failure to communicate at all. We could say that those leaders as drivers in the traffic of life are moving along the highway at night with their lights off. Others wouldn't even know they were present if not for their title on a door or listing in some organization's directory. Not communicating leaves the door open for many assumptions and does nothing to ensure that the whole team arrives at the same destination. Even if those leaders who don't communicate at all come to the people they lead and admit that they don't yet have a plan or all the answers, we could consider them decent drivers. They have communicated that there is a challenge ahead, and we could say they have their hazard lights blinking. It is far better to have hazard lights on than to continue driving along in the dark.

At the opposite end of the spectrum is the tendency to communicate like a siren. Every message that comes from you is an emergency. Eventually, no one believes anything that you say. Others lose confidence in your ability to properly communicate urgent news. Normally, when we see the flashing lights and hear the sirens of an ambulance, fire truck, or police car, we recognize this communication as an emergency. What if you always see the same emergency vehicle weaving through traffic each day with flashing lights and loud sirens, then, after moving far ahead of congested traffic, the siren fell silent? The vehicle begins moving along at the same pace as regular traffic. It would be difficult to buy into, or respect, the lights and sirens as an emergency every day. In other words, the message loses its meaningfulness and no one takes it seriously.

Being an effective communicator–one who is positive, honest, informative and clear–takes practice. You become better at it if you do it continually. Create real-life scenarios and practice what you would say in a given situation. Make sure that your horn and your lights are working.

START

Practicing in the mirror on speeches that you will give.

Role-playing with your team. For instance, practice making eye contact, better listening skills, repeating for understanding.

Joining speaking clubs like Toastmasters.

Following Stephen Covey's habit, "Listen first to understand before being understood."

Getting excited about your topic.

STOP

Ignoring the concerns of others (customers, employees, friends, and family).

Forgetting to follow-up on issues, concerns, or conversations.

Sending mixed messages; saying one thing and doing another.

Being negative every time you open your mouth.

CHAPTER TEN

Entering the Highway

(Self-Confidence)

"Some succeed because they are destined to; most succeed because they are determined to."

Anatole Fran

Experience builds self-confidence–a firm belief in yourself and your abilities. Without an accumulation of events to sharpen your skills, there is a risk that you will be shaken and doubt your own abilities. There is the danger of your buying into defeat. As tough as it may be, the best way to build confidence is to keep doing the thing that you doubt or that you're afraid of.

I remember when I was learning to drive. We would all take turns driving, and the instructor would critique what we had accomplished during the day. After days and days of practicing how to park and driving on regular streets, the day came for us to drive on the freeway. I had been driving on freeways with my parents for over a year, so this was no big deal for me. As I climbed into the driver's seat, I was confident that I could drive on the freeway.

I started to make my entrance onto the freeway; my confidence was sky high. As soon as I was about to merge into traffic, my instructor put on the brakes. You know that brake that they have installed in the floor of the passenger seat in case you are about to do something dangerous? Unfortunately, I had not seen a car that was approaching in my blind spot, and we just narrowly avoided an accident. My turn to drive was over for that day, and my confidence was diminished.

I had a talk with my father later and realized that it was better to have my confidence diminished than to have an accident and possibly have caused those of us in the car to suffer serious injuries. Still, it took some time before I regained the soaring confidence I'd had before.

It is imperative that you have confidence as a leader, or your people will have great difficulty following you. Self-confidence implies courage, and no one wants to follow a leader who is not brave.

Think back to a time in your early driving days when your time on the road was a little shaky. Think of times when you drove without your parents or guardians in the car. The first few times you were probably nervous. Naturally, you didn't want to have an accident. You were highly aware of the movements of other cars. There may have even been a time when you came to a four-way stop sign and let all the other drivers who arrived at the stop after you go through the intersection first.

But the more driving you did, the more confident you became. After a few months of driving, you took your proper turn at that four-way stop, timing the arrival of the other cars. Eventually, no one who arrived after you could proceed through the intersection before you. You used each successive experience to get better at this task and became comfortable enough to do it without doubting yourself. Then you mastered parallel parking. Then passing other cars. Then every other challenging venture on the road until you had become an expert driver.

The key thing to remember is that each event in that driving experience is a milestone, something that marked progress. You don't simply go from being uneasy to bold and confident. You take the entire journey toward confidence one juncture at a time and mark your success as you move toward an ultimate goal.

Leaders must remember to include confidence builders when setting goals for their teams. It is important for the people you lead to see larger and larger gains every step of the way. Sometimes, you will not meet your goals. But when you are able to show great improvement over previously best-demonstrated performance, you are building the confidence of individuals on your team. Your job as the leader is to recognize improvement and use that increase as a confidence builder among your people. You congratulate everyone, but let them all know you still have more work to do. Moving forward is easier because you now have a budding collective confidence to motivate everyone.

Colin Powell is an example of a leader who exhibits great self-confidence. In his autobiography, Powell credits some of his self-confidence to his career in the military. He tells how he was given the privilege of instructing new officers at The National War College shortly after he'd graduated. For him, it was an honor to be considered good enough to teach future leaders of the Army. He also says that the skills developed during his teaching days were the same skills he used when he was called upon to describe the United States' actions in the Gulf War to the American public. He mastered the art of teaching new officers, and eventually those skills transformed into teaching an entire world about war.

A more common example of confidence-building, one that millions of Americans take on daily, is weight loss. If executed properly, this process requires small milestones to reach the desired goal. However, many of us don't go about it the right way.

How many times have you heard someone say he or she wants to lose an extreme amount of weight? This plan is flawed for several reasons. For most of us, pounds are slowly shed during healthy weight loss. The effort of this plan is also tarnished by the fact that the person usually has not set any milestones. There are no opportunities for nor is there any celebrating of small successes. If your total target weight loss is fifty pounds, plan a small celebration after every ten pounds you lose.

Most leaders don't start their careers at the top of an organizational chart or in charge of an entire region or nation of people. No one goes from mailroom clerk to CEO overnight, but the small victories give you a clear path to get there. Each achievement is larger than the last, and you can begin to see what is possible. In the traffic of life, the small-scale triumphs (rounding curves, doing three-point turns) begin to build you up to achieve more demanding milestones (taking the long-distance trip on your own).

START

Repeating ten positive characteristics about yourself every morning.

Keeping a journal and writing down successes in your life daily.

Reading success stories of others.

Surrounding yourself with positive people.

Completing a goal and winning.

Practicing whatever it is you want to accomplish.

STOP

Ignoring small accomplishments; give yourself credit.

Surrounding yourself with negative people.

Taking part in negative conversations.

CHAPTER ELEVEN

Use the Feeder Road

(Change)

"If you keep doing what you've always done, you'll keep getting what you've always gotten."

Peter Francisco

If you are a healthy, active citizen of the world, there is one thing you will always encounter which is inevitable: change. The world shifts and molds itself into something new every second of the day. The way that you accept and adapt to change is a clear indicator of how successful you can be in the midst of those shifts. Not accepting change is a guarantee for insanity. What is insanity? It's doing the same thing over and over again and expecting different results. As is clear in the following account, you almost always have a secondary choice. A leader is always prepared to activate an alternate plan.

I was in five o'clock traffic and cars were bumper to bumper. The day was hot and humid and I was trying to think of another route that would get me home faster. I was in the far left lane, and as I glanced over at the lane beside me I noticed that it was starting to move much faster. Since my lane was not moving, I wondered if there was an accident in my lane or just idiots who were unable to drive in traffic. I immediately switched lanes because I thought I would get ahead of the people in my lane and outsmart the grind of five o'clock traffic. However, once I'd made the lane change I was now bumper-to-bumper in that lane. Moreover, the car I was behind in my original lane now passed me by. How frustrating!

I second-guessed my decision and switched back into my original lane. The time was now five-thirty, and I realized I was not making any progress switching from lane to lane. I decided to make a change by exiting the freeway. I struggled at first with that decision because I observed a few other people exiting and I did not want to get stuck on the feeder road. The decision to change proved to be a success. I was moving faster than the cars on the freeway.

Sometimes you have to have the courage to follow the path of change. Go willingly and trust your ability to come up with new strategies. If life is serving you a challenge and you are not making progress, you should be willing to exit the freeway and try something different. It is also your responsibility as a leader to guide others to change if they, too, seem to be falling short of their goals. Nothing is worse in the midst of change than repeated failure of a plan. This, of course, does not mean the people following the plan are failures. It is merely the plan that fails. Often people lose confidence in their own abilities during change; what they should doubt is the outdated plan that is obviously not leading to worthwhile progress.

A trip over unknown terrain can be slippery. The human urge is to always know everything ahead of time. Logically, this is impossible. We don't know everything. The best we can hope for ourselves is that we recognize what we know and are willing to learn what we don't. It is healthy to embrace the unknown. Own it. It tests your ability to emerge more knowledgeable from challenge. Accept that you don't know everything, and move forward using everything that you do know.

You can't always anticipate change before it arrives. Keith Harrell says in his book "Attitude Is Everything" that "Change can be planned or unplanned." What you can anticipate, though, is your ability to be flexible when you must undergo the inevitable shifts that will occur in your life. Keep your clarity during those times. Having the vision to promote and accept change will foster an environment that inspires creative solutions. If you don't *change with change*, you minimize millions of opportunities to chase success.

Think again about the account above when the driver changed his route and took the feeder road. He was determined not to sit in traffic all day. After several lane changes that resulted in failure, he finally decided to try something different by exiting the freeway. Some drivers would have remained in traffic and never considered other ways to get to their destination. If that driver's goal was to make it home in a certain amount of time, he could not use the same route at the onset of heavy traffic. He had to find another solution—whether he teamed up with a friend and took the HOV lane, used the toll road, or caught a subway or bus, he had to find another solution since the original plan was not working.

We can think of the need to be willing to change as a detour sign. Even though the detour signs point us toward a different route, we still end up at our desired destination. Life will present you with countless detour signs. As a leader, you must recognize when it's time to detour and when you can stay on course. In the traffic of life, making the decision to exit onto a feeder road is a critical moment. It is one in which you weigh your options, and it requires risk. It may not be the popular thing to do if there aren't very many cars doing the same. The alternative may be bumper-to-bumper traffic and an arrival time that is far later than the time you wanted to get home. Be willing to not follow the masses. Risk change. Know that any hint of failure is not personal failure. It's the way to adapt to new shifts in your world.

Now what if you exit onto the feeder road and the weather begins to turn severe? Or there is a sudden heavy downpour of rain? The first area to flood is likely to be that feeder road. Guess what? You are still in the process of exploring a change and you still have other options. You can even return to the freeway, since most feeder roads take you through one red light and allow you access back onto the freeway. What is important is that you take the chance to investigate the prospect of change when the moment presents itself. Don't miss the opportunity. There are many others who will take the risk, find something new that works and, eventually, clear the way for others to do the same. Those people are leaders. They don't fear taking an exit and know that sometimes one may be pleasantly surprised at where a feeder road can lead.

START

Trying what works for others and see if it will work for you.

Writing down what you want to change about yourself. Set a time frame.

Remaining flexible.

Acting immediately. Motivation is temporary.

STOP

Giving up if you fail the first time.

Continuing to make the same mistakes. Change something.

Going back to old routines that are outdated.

Harboring a "My way or the highway" attitude. Be open to suggestions.

Thinking that technology can't help.

CHAPTER TWELVE

The Radio

(Relationships)

"I don't know the key success, but the key to failure is trying to please everyone.

Bill Cosby

It may be difficult to believe, but the human psyche is easily programmed. Your ability to think, feel and reason is directly affected by whom and what you choose to surround yourself with. This includes both people and your environmental influences–books, music, paintings or images in your home, the internet. Because the American public spends an inordinate amount of time being fed informational bytes by the media, television and radio have become two of our most dominant influences. Drive time in a car is a very important time of influence for most people:

> *When I was a young man, I listened to my favorite Houston, Texas, radio stations, KSBJ and KMJQ. I could repeat the words to almost every song in the top ten countdown. Whatever was on the radio on the way to work was the topic of my conversations for that day. I could not function without my radio. I listened to the music, news, weather, and sports reports. As I grew older, my passion for music diminished, and I developed a love for talk radio. My favorite talk radio station is Houston's Sports Radio 610 and the Jim Rhome Show. I can remember laughing aloud in my car as I listened to this show. I'm sure people who passed me wondered, "What drug is he on?" I also listened to every other sports radio host that was on the air while I was driving.*

The truth is, influence is a drug. From the moment that you begin taking in the words and sounds and actions of others via any medium, you move into an altered state, a state of receptivity. You allow yourself to be educated or entertained–shaped and molded– by what you see, hear, smell, taste, touch, or perceive. It's amazing how people can influence our lives and how the things we hear daily can consume our thoughts and become a part of our behavior. This is precisely how slang, rumors, public opinion, or public fear all spread throughout a population. It *influences* its way among us.

The radio can become your best friend and personal coach. If you listen to something every day, eventually it will begin to influence how you think and what you talk about. So, the question becomes: Who and what is influencing your life? Who is your radio that you listen to each day?

It seems almost cliché to say here that your "radio" influences need to be positive ones, but we'll say it. Negativity is highly contagious and can infect you with the slightest influence. It ensures your overall health suffers and impedes your progress. If your radio is always spewing negative talk (people who tear you down rather than build you up, people who doubt your goals, whiners and complainers who are always expressing their discontent at how life has handed them an unfair deal), some of it will rub off on you. Misery loves company, so you should be very selective about the company you keep. You don't want miserable company. Make sure the relationships you build are positive for both you and the other people vested in them.

You are on your way to becoming the very people with whom you surround yourself. Perhaps this is easier to grasp if you envision yourself and the people you associate with as houses and properties. You must be careful where you build. If you wanted to build a million-dollar home you would not consider building it in a sixty thousand-dollar neighborhood. You want your property value to increase to over a million, not decrease to sixty thousand. As a leader, what is your property value at your workplace? Are you the million-dollar home or one of the sixty thousand-dollar homes? How are you increasing your property value?

At some point during your consumption of radio, you must learn to balance everything that you take in. An inner voice, one with its own opinions and values independent of everyone else's, must kick in. That voice must monitor new influences against your own value system. In order to do this effectively, there must be a limit on how much influence comes into your life. Too much of anything can be a bad thing. Create balance. Make choices about how much of an influence from certain people, from certain radio stations; you need in your life. The good thing about radio is that you can choose your channels. You can tune in to stations that keep you informed about current events, favorite sports team, economical issues, or issues that entertain and enlighten you. Choose the people in your life in the same manner. Select friends who are good for you, who influence you positively. Select yourself, too, when you are positive. Self-talk is equally a positive, healthy influence. It gives you a chance to reinforce your goals and motivate yourself by reiterating what it is you're working toward. It develops you as a leader by stimulating you to believe in what you're doing.

The brain is like a computer: The data you input will reflect what you output. Listening to positive radio–optimistic friends, associates, and others who can add to the betterment of you as a person–is essential to good leadership. Tune into the things that uplift you, not the things that habitually weigh you down.

START

Listening to "self-help" tapes versus the radio station.

Associating with people who are positive and share your common beliefs.

Getting involved with support groups that are doing what you aspire to do.

Making relationship calls—phone calls to key members in an organization who can help you achieve your goals.

STOP

Tolerating negative influences in your life.

Letting the failures of others dictate your potential successes.

Letting one person influence you so much that you are no longer the person you want to be.

CHAPTER THIRTEEN

Getting Over

(Persistence)

*"Determined people make conditions.
They do not allow themselves to be victims
of them."*

Jim Casey

Opportunity is a very small opening. When it presents itself you must take it. You must pursue it with a determination that won't let you turn back. Here's how one driver had to stay determined in order to make his turn:

I was leaving my house and about to enter the freeway during five o'clock traffic. As soon as I entered the entry ramp to the freeway and made my way to the center, I saw cars at a complete standstill. The traffic was terrible and it was hot, so I attempted to get over into the next lane. When I placed my signal light on to get over, the car on the side of me increased his speed and moved up to ensure that I could not get over. I knew this was about to turn into a battle as I continued trying to get over into the next lane.

My driving instructor had told me to always communicate in traffic by using my signal light when I wanted to get over. I thought I would never get another chance after I missed my first opportunity. My exit was approaching soon, and I knew I had to get over or drive three miles to the next exit. Each time I signaled, another car would speed up in the lane that I needed to get into. Finally, I decided not to use my signal light. When the next opening presented itself, I would take it. The space between the cars was tight, but I saw an opening and I got over in time to make my exit.

This driver was persistent. There was only a small window of opportunity, and he had to time it just right in order to make his turn. Other drivers blocked his attempts to reach his exit. He persevered in spite of interference and ill treatment. No matter how frustrated he became, he persisted–in fact, *insisted*–until his break came.

In the traffic of life, you have to be willing to be this persistent to achieve any significant goal in your life. Otherwise, you could lose sight of your goals. What if you are trying to make your cost goals or improve your service at your company? You cannot simply give up if the first quarter does not go your way. If it's a promotion that you are chasing, don't give up if you're not selected in the first or second round. Perhaps it will take you four or five attempts to finally be promoted. Maybe you will land it in your third attempt, but you'll never know if you give up in the second round. Persistence is all about not letting challenges distract you. If the driver trying to get over to take his exit had given in to the emotion of the moment (frustration), he might not have keep a cool enough demeanor to calculate the lane change and move over safely. Persistence leads to what some people would call *luck*. It's amazing how many "lucky" hard-working people we have in this world. (Ha!) The truth is they are persistent. They have accumulated a wealth of experience through their perseverance alone. The more experience you have, the luckier you get. Luck, then, is where experience meets opportunity.

As you establish your goals, it is important to remember that opportunity will not always present itself to you as a gift. When the driver put on his signal and informed everyone of his goal to get over into the exit lane, he faced a lot of resistance. Other drivers seemed to be outright protesting his decision by speeding up and not allowing him to merge in front of them. However, when he turned his signal light off and seized an opportunity, he was able to get over.

Not everyone will be receptive or supportive when you make your goal known. If you choose to disclose it, remember that there may be others who will do everything in their power to block your opportunities. You can't always sit back and wait for opportunity to appear and hope someone signals you to get over simply because you've communicated what you want. You may be waiting for the rest of your life. You may experience more opposition than you ever have before ... and from the people you'd hoped would be more supportive.

In traffic, how many times do people actually let you get over into the next lane? In most cases, you have to be persistent and make an opportunity for yourself. Decide you are going to make your goal happen even if the other cars won't support you. If you see there is not enough room between your car and the car in front of you, keep inching into the lane until you force your way in. You don't quit, or shy away from your original goal. You *must* get over.

Be persistent enough to wear the resistors down; don't let them wear you down. Believe that you will succeed under any conditions. After all, the chance to change lanes is not always granted to the one who drives the fastest, but to the one who keeps on driving.

START

Identifying one goal and promising yourself, "I will not quit until I achieve this goal."

Reading success stores on people who never gave up on their dreams despite facing several obstacles.

Repeating this quote daily "Quitting is a permanent solution to a temporary problem."

Looking in the mirror every morning and stating, "I am a winner. I will not quit on my family, my values, my dreams, or myself."

STOP

Saying "It just wasn't meant to be."

Doubting your talents.

Letting "isms" determine your outcome (racism, sexism, ageism, etc.)

CHAPTER FOURTEEN

The Right Vehicle

(Delegating)

"Every job is a self-portrait of the person who did it. Autograph your work with excellence."

Anonymous

You are only as strong as the people you lead. Your leadership should inspire every single person to be a leader, rather than merely your follower. In fact, some of the best-run organizations are those in which every member of a team is qualified to run the team in the absence of the leader. Good leadership inspires every team player to be prepared to rise to the challenge if called.

Have you ever been on a road trip from hell? I remember in college taking a road trip to a football game. I was outvoted on taking a van to the game. I thought it was a great idea so that we could all ride together. However, the others wanted to drive their own cars so that they would be free after the game to leave and have a good time.

We decided on a meeting place on campus and waited for everyone to arrive. Then we all piled into several cars and followed each other through town. Along the way, we tried to keep up with the lead car. Sometimes we were forced to run traffic lights to keep up with the pack. In the beginning, it seemed like this was going to be a fun trip. The radio was blasting, we were excited about the game, and there was fun waiting for us in Dallas.

By the time we left Austin, our convoy consisted of five cars with my car as the lead. This lasted until one car sped up and pulled ahead of mine, indicating with blinking lights that they needed to make a stop. We exited the highway, now following a new lead car. Some complained about the time; others got food; some got gas. After about twenty minutes, we got back in our cars. In the next thirty miles, another car would speed up and take the lead. We got on and off the highway again numerous times.

It was getting close to game time. As we drove into Dallas, we realized no one really knew where the stadium was. We all knew the general area. We looked at a city map and rode around following the directions of anyone who said they knew where the stadium was. Basically, we drove in circles and wasted a lot of time. Everyone knew where to go but no one knew how to get there. No one was in charge, and everyone was trying to do everything. We finally made it to the game two minutes before kickoff, but it remains one of the most challenging road trips I have ever taken.

How could this trip have been better? The first lead car could have remained the lead car, deciding on times for food, gas, or stretching, and a delegate from each car could have been designated to obtain food for that particular car. The lead car driver would have been the one to call all drivers to remind them to fill up before leaving town. He would have set the time to meet and head out.

But no matter how hard we tried, it was nearly impossible to get four cars filled with college students to a football game without their participation and help. Think about it. How realistic is it to expect so many people to buy food and gas, find directions, and arrive on time if everyone does not collaborate on the plan? Because they did not come together to map out a plan that involved everyone's special talents, the trip was a disaster. Each stop slowed them down more. Frustration levels grew high as they noticed that the game was about to start. Delegation and teamwork might have prevented the tension that mounted as the students rode around looking for the stadium.

In the traffic of life, it is important to delegate. No one can do it all. No one person is an expert because he has acquired all of his knowledge alone in a vacuum. A true leader knows when to delegate responsibilities and how to place the right person in charge of certain tasks. At an auto repair shop, each mechanic is a specialist on one part or function of the car. Someone knows about the transmission. The tire specialist knows about rotating and balancing tires. You won't find the tire specialist working on the transmission. Be wary of any repair shop with one person specializing in everything. It does not necessarily mean that he can't perform all the functions that he advertises. He may be an efficient one-man show. But if he specializes in everything, it might mean that he excels at nothing. Would he be as efficient and timely as Jiffy Lube on oil changes or Discount Tire Co. on the tires? Leaders, likewise, are not experts at everything and must know when to delegate to the "specialists" on their team.

To delegate, by definition, is "to commit or entrust to another." A leader authorizes someone else as the responsible party. He is placing the control of that particular event in someone else's hands. Delegating is not an easy task because if the event he is entrusting to someone else is not successful, he is ultimately still responsible. A good leader, however, uses this to his or her advantage.

Don't misunderstand delegating. It does not mean letting everyone else do all of the work. It does mean accepting that in order to get all of the work done, you may need to share the responsibilities. This does not lessen a leader's participation. Delegating requires effective planning, an efficiency tool. One large project becomes several small projects that are easier to execute. It simply makes a large project easier to manage.

The true test of delegating lies in the results and accomplishments through the team's efforts. It requires the leader to first acknowledge the size of the situation and to prepare a plan of action. He then chooses those who will carry out his plan. He must know who is capable of what in order to ensure that the results are promising.

Delegating is a must in a busy life; and most leaders lead extremely busy lives. We all have families, church functions, meetings, weekend obligations and must somehow figure out how to get everything done. Zig Ziglar once asked, "How do you eat an elephant?" The answer, quite simply, is "One bite at a time." The leader takes that elephant–the big project at hand–and he slices it into tiny pieces. He hands those pieces to the team and, in no time, that elephant is digested. The team is full and satisfied. Without ever even realizing how big the project, goal, or problem was, they just ate it. And the leader has done his job. He has successfully accomplished his goal with the help of his entire team.

So, how do you begin to delegate? Choose the right people for the right task. Take the time to learn the skills and talents of those on your team or in your group. Develop the skills of those who need help. Make sure your weakest link is also strong. The only way to accomplish that is by giving the extra attention to the entire team so that *everyone* is capable of being a valuable contributor.

When you learn to delegate, your efficiency levels rise. You save time, manage resources, and make the world of your team ripe for stress-free achievement. Understand that not everyone is good at everything, including you, the leader. But everyone has at least one talent or strength that can benefit the whole team. There is an old saying that goes: "If you want something done right, then do it yourself." Leave room for a new saying: "If you want something done right, get the right people to do it."

START

Selecting the right people for the right job.

Assigning roles and responsibilities.

Using a calendar to assign tasks to others and set completion dates.

Developing people so you can delegate.

STOP

Trying to do everything yourself.

Believing that only you are capable of doing it right.

Distrusting teammates to complete assigned tasks.

Believing you will lose the credit.

CHAPTER FIFTEEN

Back Seat Driver

(Experience)

"Learn from the mistakes of others. You won't live long enough to make them all yourself."

Anonymous

The most important realization you can have as a human is that you are a lifelong learner. Even if you are a leader, someone who historically teaches things to other people, you benefit from the experience of others. It only improves the quantity of things you are qualified to teach to other people. Experience amounts to how much you've been able to learn. Here's what new knowledge one driver discovered was unexpectedly waiting for her ... from her husband:

I was driving one day in traffic, heading towards downtown Houston. It was a beautiful day, and I was meeting my husband for lunch at one of our favorite restaurants. I had timed everything just right and had made it through most of the traffic. I took my usual exit and headed north. This is what I had always done. However, when I arrived at Main Street, there was a detour. I could only make a right turn. It led to a dead end or onto another street that only turned left.

As I traveled through the maze of detour signs, I was wasting a lot of time. I was going to be late for lunch. I finally made it back to Main Street, but now I was six blocks past where I needed to be. To make a very long trip through downtown short, I made it to lunch half an hour late.

When I arrived, my husband gave me this look that said, "How could you be late to a restaurant that we have been meeting at for the past year? You must know how to get here by now." As I told him about the detour signs and all of the closed streets, he said, "All you had to do was exit Travis Street and make a right. That takes you around the construction and directly to the parking lot of the restaurant." Of course I gave him a look of my own. If I had known that, dear, before I took my regular exit, I would have been here on time.

Experience is what he had that I did not. If I had known that from his daily commute downtown he knew about the construction and all of the detours before my trip, I would have made it to lunch on time. He never thought to tell me, and I never thought to ask him. Having already taken the route gave him valuable experience that I did not have. From this point forward, though, I would know about the detours. Unfortunately, knowing this now didn't sweeten the mood of our time at the restaurant. Needless to say, it was a short lunch.

Everyone benefits from the experience of others. There is always someone who has done something before you and knows it better. Fearlessly pursuing the experience of others is a time-saver. You avoid so many unnecessary mistakes. You give yourself the benefit of seeing a situation before it happens through the eyes of someone who has already been through it.

Here's another example. Suppose you are driving in traffic behind an eighteen-wheeler or big SUV? You notice the driver puts his blinker on to get over into another lane. You are pleased. Once that car moves you speed up only to find that you are now behind another car that has a blinking light on. That car moves into the next lane, and you speed up again behind yet another car. Finally you are home free and drive about five feet before your lane dead-ends into an orange barrier cone. You now have to come almost to a complete stop to get over. You couldn't have known for sure what was ahead of you. However, you were so anxious to get around slower cars that you paid no attention to the fact that they were all moving into another lane. These cars had had the experience of seeing that orange cone and knowing to move over. You didn't take advantage of that experience.

What if you are driving through a neighborhood with which you're not familiar? Perhaps you are visiting a friend's home for the first time. He has warned you to take it easy over the huge speed bumps that were just constructed near his house. You travel the normal speed limit of thirty miles an hour through the residential area when you suddenly hear a loud thump. The car goes airborne for a couple of seconds and you realize you just hit the biggest speed bump you've ever seen in your life. You did not heed your friend's warning. His knowledge and experience might have benefited you had you taken it seriously enough to follow it. The next time you visit him you will probably drive slower than thirty miles per hour.

The experience of others only helps you if you act on it. To act means to do. Once they pass it on to you, you have the obligation to make it yours.

Leaders whose networks and social circles are comprised of people from all walks of life and with all types of experience benefit in many ways. Both their short- and long-term goals are affected as some teammates may have immediate solutions to problems from their own experience. Think of the thousands of entrepreneurial pioneers who have laid the foundation for millions of businesses in the world. From Sam Walton of Wal-Mart to Bill Gates of Microsoft, business leaders have developed a blueprint of success through both their accomplishments and their mistakes. Anyone who wants to build a better prototype of Wal-Mart or Microsoft already has a sturdy foundation. You only have to build upon what has been started. Use readily available resources–the internet, books, libraries, software–to learn more about the experiences of others. Study the craft of experience. Minimize errors by learning from the mistakes of others. Learn the traffic of life detours. Know which roads come to a dead end and which ones will get you where you're going on time.

START

Learning from others who have gone before you.

Enlisting a mentor for you or your team.

Studying trends in your organization.

Researching your industry and learning about its history.

Reading success stories of people who've faced similar challenges.

STOP

Thinking only you have all the answers.

Ignoring input from those with more life experience.

Continuing to make the same mistakes. Ask how it should or could be done better.

CHAPTER SIXTEEN

The Yellow Light

(Opportunities)

"You miss 100% of the shots you never take."

Wayne Gretzky

A yellow light is an opportunity to take a chance. You know there is a small window of opportunity to make it through the light before it becomes red (and illegal). Yellow does not mean stop. It tells you to proceed with caution. Here's a story from a driver who got a thrill from yellow lights (and was annoyed at a missed opportunity to drive through them):

It was Friday morning, and I had a major presentation to give at work on the characteristics of leadership. When I got in my car, I had an extra thirty minutes to spare. I approached the leg of my daily commute that usually delays me the most. This street contains more than fifteen traffic lights, but leads directly to the entrance of my job. I liked to get in front of the line of cars so that I could make the proper decision on each light. It was fun to treat this part of my day as a game, and I was determined to make this day one of my best finishes.

I approached my first traffic light, and it was already green. As I proceeded to the next light, the game was on. I traveled at just the right speed in the middle lane to catch each light. I was making good progress ... and then it happened. I looked over my left shoulder and the car in the next lane was trying to get in front of me. I noticed the expression on that driver's face and realized he was playing the same game of beat the lights that I was; only somehow he got in front of me and was starting to slow down. The light ahead was still green, but I was getting nervous we would miss the light. The speed of the all the cars in the middle lane began to be altered because that lead car had slowed down. The light was now yellow. I just knew the car ahead of me would not make us lose the game. To my disappointment, the driver of the car stopped at the yellow light, fearful it would turn red and he would be in violation. I was angry. My game had come to an end, and I missed my opportunity to catch all the lights for the first time.

While it is best to be safe and know that proceeding through a yellow light will not cause an accident or violate a traffic rule, sometimes you must be willing to go through the yellow light. It takes you out of a comfort zone and pushes you to take a risk. Often, you have only a split second to make a decision about it before the light is red and you can no longer cross under the light. But once the light turns red, you are invariably one of the cars left behind.

By no means is there any suggestion here to break the law and run a red light. You risk being sideswiped and injuring yourself and other drivers. What we mean to suggest is that leaders take the chance while the light is still yellow. They take advantage of an opportunity while it still exists. Sometimes if you quibble too long and belabor a decision, you miss the shot of a lifetime. You then have to redirect your goals.

Many success stories are based on the lives of people who have known when to go through a yellow light. They take chances when others will not. They are willing to remove themselves from a mode of ease and venture into uncertain frontiers. Stopping means they might never have known what was possible after they passed through the yellow light. And sometimes, the adrenaline you receive by just pressing through that yellow light is motivation enough to keep driving.

Have you ever passed a driver appearing nervous who was stopped at a yellow light? They might have been late for work, a big date, or late picking up the kids from school ... they're just late, period. The millionaires and successful people in this world are those who went through the yellow light and did not fear the consequences. They didn't fear the impact of another car; they didn't make room for failure or humiliation.

There is a saying that one cannot find a new horizon unless he leaves the shore. There is a certain beauty and boldness that comes with not knowing what lies ahead for you and moving ahead anyway. One of the reasons so many people are intrigued (mesmerized) with basketball superstar Michael Jordan is because of his success at taking the last shot to win games. The clock ticks down to its final seconds (Yellow light! Yellow light!) and he is still willing to shoot the ball. He risks it all to make the winning point.

New horizons will not come to you unless you are willing to proceed through the yellow lights of your life. Leaders must be willing to do so for themselves and for their teams. If your team is counting on you to take a chance on that big project, and you stop at every yellow light, your team stops with you. You are crushing an opportunity for others. Even if you can't justify the advantage of proceeding through a yellow light, and your team still wants to go, it is up to you to take the chance. How many people do you know who won't make a big presentation, or turn down opportunities to meet the boss, or never voice an opinion in any meeting ... all because they don't want to risk going through a yellow light?

This book is a yellow light. Writing it has taken us, the authors, out of a comfort zone and required us to risk the chance that someone wants to read (and believe in) what we have to say. There is the possibility that no one will even care about these words, or that what we've written may fail to move any reader to a higher state of awareness. We wrote it anyway, despite the possibility of failure. It moves us aggressively through the yellow light and guarantees this opportunity will not have passed us by. When your yellow light presents itself, don't be afraid to keep driving.

START

Accepting all opportunities to speak or lead, key projects.

Thinking outside the box.

Getting others involved and do some brainstorming.

Keeping up with technological changes and advances.

Believing in yourself.

STOP

Walking away when your boss comes around.

Thinking your way is the only way and you must have all the answers.

Getting the same negative results and not attempting to change because it's the way you have always done things.

CHAPTER SEVENTEEN

Carpooling

(Teamwork)

"Success is a team effort. If you can't put people up, please don't put them down"

NASA slogan

When the concept of carpooling came into vogue, it was the mid-seventies and the price of gas had skyrocketed. Our country's leaders were trying to come up with ways to reduce our dependency on imported oil. Long lines at the gas pumps were common. For families, carpooling meant more trips with relatives. At its most fundamental level, carpooling was employed to get our nation through the gas crisis. But what it forced us to do as a whole during this period was to form a team to combat the situation in which the oil embargo had placed us.

In major cities today, the purpose of carpooling has shifted. We do it now to try to minimize traffic, save money, and save the environment. The carpooling system has become structured with sophisticated rewards, such as high-occupancy vehicle (HOV) lanes that allow drivers to move faster in traffic. What hasn't changed about carpooling is that it still forces us (as citizens) to act as teams.

A team is a squad of people who work together toward a common goal. As a leader, your job is to nurture cooperation among your people. As you assemble the members of your team, several factors are key: How well are you prepared as a leader to motivate others to accomplish the team goals? Does the team believe the goal can be accomplished? Do the team members know their role on the team? Do all team members benefit from accomplishing the goal? Have the team members bought into the leader's goals?

After you have assessed these things for your team, it is important to establish a protocol for communication. Decide upon the rules of exchange. Will you have regular written communication or face-to-face meetings with your team? Will you meet one-on-one or as an assembly? Is there special language that you will use to convey specific meanings to your team? The reason this is important to decide is because it sets a standard for trust. If team members know you will update them at the same time each week, they trust that time with you as an opportunity to build. It places everyone on the same page because you will all be speaking the same language. Establish the infrastructure of your communication channels and then remain consistent with it. It makes it easy to deliver information and sets parameters for the way that your team members communicate with each other.

One of the best examples of a team working together to reach a common goal occurs in the pit crew of a fast-growing American pastime: NASCAR. Here the drivers pull into the pit area after racing at speeds of up to 190 miles per hour. They get their tires changed, windows cleaned, and a full tank of gas in less than twelve seconds. The teamwork required is tremendous. Most of what observers see is the teamwork; they make it look easy, so we don't give the team as much credit for accomplishing its job so flawlessly. But you can imagine what would happen if the driver pulled off with only three tires. NASCAR championships are often won or lost based on what happens in the pit area. The passion of the crew leader gets transferred to his team. He has a vision that everyone has been able to buy into. Subsequently, the passion of the crew members carries the power to determine the outcome of a race.

We don't all follow the NASCAR circuit, but we all, by virtue of being human, run some kind of race on a daily basis. In the movie *Remember the Titans,* the coach, played by Denzel Washington, offers great lessons in team-building. The story takes place in Virginia during a time when schools were into desegregation to combat the strain of race relations. The coach takes two high school football teams—one black, the other white—and morphs them into one champion team. He takes the combined team to a training camp and instills in them the belief that they can be champions.

Though it becomes a tough road to travel, the players manage to become a winning team, learning both life lessons and invaluable things about each other. Mostly, they learn that beneath the racial divide, we are all humans with similar needs and sensibilities. But these young men learn, too, that people with different backgrounds can work tirelessly for the same goal.

One of the reasons that the *Titans* example works is because the players bought into the coach's vision. Eventually, each of them had a personal investment in winning. They each had a voice in the decision-making process and were able to buy in without reservation. People invest fully in the ideas or processes that value their participation.

As a leader, you have many ways to accomplish this buy-in factor. Have brainstorm meetings and solicit feedback from team members. Get team members to make personal sacrifices so that they invest and have the possibility of a return. Make personal sacrifices yourself to show your team members that you are committed. Something as simple as giving an employee a day off and carrying his load in his absence shows a team that you are willing to give up something for the common goal.

When you step into the role of leader for a team, you must consider the length of time the team has been in existence. There is a team history that begins the moment everyone comes together, and the growth of the entire unit goes through several critical phases. Although there is some necessary chemistry that must develop for a team to evolve into efficient units, it takes time for the chemistry to become *right*. But new teams that enjoy early successes find it easy for the confidence of the team to grow. They find the niches that make them a unique collection of talents. They learn to be the pit crew that wins races. Early successes give them something to look back on and something to look forward to.

START

Listening to your team.

Setting group goals.

Having group activities where all members participate.

Identifying informal leaders and defining the roles of each team member.

Recognizing each member's accomplishments.

Having fun.

STOP

Delaying performance results.

Sending mixed messages.

Changing the rules. Have them defined.

CHAPTER EIGHTEEN

Shade Tree Mechanics

(Education)

"When we do more than we are paid to do, eventually we will be paid more for what we do."

Zig Ziglar

Opportunities for learning await you around every corner. You must be willing to invest in them. Sometimes that investment may seem pricey, but as the following driver discovered, in the end a good education is worth every dime you pay for it.

Instinctively, I knew it was not going to be a good day. While cruising at fifty-five miles per hour down the highway on my way to work, all of the lights on my dashboard came on. Fortunately, I was able to coast over to the shoulder and call a co-worker to pick me up and take me to work. My co-worker asked me if I knew what was wrong with my car and all I could do was shake my head no. I was clueless. I had had my car for about five years, and it was beginning to show age. I was spending more and more time at repair shops, and I knew that I was going to have to spend some money to get it fixed again.

After arriving at work, I began searching for a mechanic. Over the years, I had several mechanics repair my vehicle. Usually, I picked the cheapest one to try to save money. Invariably, the same problems would crop up over and over again.

This time, I decided to try a mechanic who specialized in European cars. After having my vehicle towed to the mechanic I had selected, he told me over the phone that it sounded like a six hundred dollar job, but he would have to inspect the car first. Later that day, I called to get the bad news. Much to my surprise, he told me that there would be no charge because the problem was only a loose wire.

For the first time in my life, I had not used a shade tree mechanic—nicknamed as such based on their reputation for working under the shade of a tree rather than out of a professional garage. These types of mechanics could usually fix your car, but they had no formal training or education. Sometimes their diagnosis of the problem would be hit or miss. Many times I had spent money to get something repaired without solving the original problem, but what *else should I have expected? I was using the services of someone who had not invested enough in his own education to educate me.*

This time I had chosen a specialty mechanic with some knowledge of repairing cars like mine, and the entire experience was free. I received an important education that day. From that day forward, I stopped using those shade tree mechanics and started taking my car to someone who was properly prepared to do the right thing by me.

Education is priceless, no matter how much it costs. One of the best bumper stickers ever created says, "If you think the price of an education is high, try not getting one." In the case of the driver trying to decide whether to use a shade tree mechanic, someone was able to avoid a problem that didn't even exist.

Leaders must constantly seek out educational opportunities that help them grow personally and professionally. They should be advocates for education and find ways to develop themselves and their teams. Leaders who don't believe education is constant and ongoing often believe they have all the answers and don't take learning new things seriously. What they don't realize is that when they stop learning they stop growing.

Think back to the driver's education class you took in high school. You learned many rules that you would not have, had you merely counted on one of your parents to teach you how to drive. It's not that your parents would have done a poor job of teaching you to drive. Their driving experiences gave them much comfort with navigating the road. They already knew many of the rules you needed to learn. However, as a new driver with no experiences to count on, you needed a more formal education to be certain you covered all the things that you are required by law to know. Think of all the things you have to be concerned about as a new driver. Teaching you about all those things was too large a task for the loving nurture of your parents. You needed a firmer hand, someone who had been trained to give you both nurturing and hard-core instruction.

In today's competitive society, some type of formal education is a minimum requirement for success. This education does not have to be in a college setting, but it is necessary to give you an edge above competitors. Some would-be leaders believe they don't have time to go back to school. If this is your excuse, then you believe this to your own detriment. If you are not learning, you probably will not be earning what you could be worth. An education makes you more valuable and far more marketable. If you get a job teaching new drivers how to drive, people are willing to pay a certain amount of money for that service. However, if you are teaching tractor-trailer drivers how to pull big rigs, your level of education has to be higher. The skill-set you develop to teach someone to drive tractor-trailers is much more involved. You can expect to be paid more than a regular driving instructor.

Beyond educating yourself, as a leader you also have a responsibility to educate your team. A team's education is an important part of a leader's job. You can bring in outside speakers to motivate your team and help with their personal development. You can suggest a book for everyone to read and discuss the merits of it with the group. You can choose to train and develop the team yourself. Whether it's a class, seminar, book, or tape, educational opportunities plant seeds for achieving goals.

It is important to remember that education is not always solely formal. There are life lessons that can't be imparted through a college or university career. Many people have walls covered with college degrees, but no life experience–book smart, but common-sense deficient. On the converse, some of the most successful people in the world have never attended any prestigious school or university; they are successful because they maximized their educational opportunities. When life taught them a lesson, they paid attention and built on that experience.

If you are a leader who does not continue to educate yourself, there are domino-effect consequences for your life. Your team may lose its motivation because your lack of education makes them believe you are incompetent. A team that loses its motivation can also lose its direction. If the team loses direction, your response to them may become reactionary and extreme. The death blow to the team eventually comes. They all agree that you are an ineffective leader.

To avoid these downfalls, education needs to be a primary pursuit. When you place it low on your priority list, what you pay for can mean the success or failure of your entire career.

START

Continuing your education by investing in yourself.

Reading. Select at least one book per month.

Learning from life experiences. "Don't make the same mistake twice."

Developing others to educate themselves on their craft.

STOP

Waiting for someone to bring you the answer.

Wasting time. Watching too much television can deter you from achieving.

Trying to learn it all yourself. Get a mentor.

CHAPTER NINETEEN

Flat Tires

(Patience)

"The road to success has many tempting parking places."

Steve Potter

A flat tire is a test. It tries your ability to find a way to move on or give in to a standstill. You pass or fail this test depending on your resolve. Do you give up or find another way to make yourself mobile?

It seems at times that tires go flat when you are cutting it close to making a meeting or important engagement. You know that no one at your meeting will believe you. The flat tire excuse is the oldest one in the book. You want to know: *Why me? Why at this moment?* The truth is there is no *best time* for a flat tire. If you drive a car, a flat tire comes with the territory. The wear and tear of driving assures it. You don't plan for it; it's one of those things that is bound to happen sooner or later.

When it happens, you have a choice before you. Are you going to let it continue to delay you or are you going to try to do something about it? The prospect of doing something about it may not thrill you. How many people get excited about changing a flat tire? But you have to resolve this situation if you ever hope to arrive where you're going. This is not a permanent obstacle. It is merely a delay. And you'll need a healthy dose of patience in order to remove this temporary barrier and change that tire.

The power to change your circumstance rests squarely on your willingness to be invincible. You have to want more than anything in that moment to ride again. You know that this fix won't require any leap into a drastic measure. You won't need to buy a new car. You only need to change the tire. You know that you need to tap your resource pool if it is not something you can do yourself. It is not a requirement of leadership that you have all the skills or all the answers to fix every problem that you encounter. That may lead you to a faulty decision-making process. You can call someone who is skilled at fixing flats. Or you might even consider using Fix-A-

Flat on the tire as a temporary solution or use a half spare rather than a full spare.

Fix-A-Flat is not a display of patience. Rather, it is a quick-fix solution to the problem. If you use Fix-A-Flat, realize you will only be putting a band-aid on an open gash. Leaders cannot afford to fall prey to this type of thinking when their employees, spouses, and organizations identify a concern. They must be willing to invest the time that will address the issue properly.

The point of emphasizing that you deal with the flat in *some* way which is amenable to your current predicament is to say that you know in your mind this is a setback that is completely conquerable. If you stay steadfast on the path to fixing it, you could be on the way to your meeting in a matter of moments, especially if you have a spare in your trunk and an immediate plan to get it on the car. And if you are a leader with a truly indomitable spirit, you might even consider riding on that flat, passing several repair stations, to make your meeting and worry about fixing it later.

In the traffic of life, some people realize they have a flat tire and have no plan to fix it. They don't even acknowledge it. For example, if you know your attitude is causing you to perform poorly at your job, don't ignore it. Treat it like a flat. Change the tire and keep moving.

One of your charges as a leader is also to inspire the patience in your constituents so that they, too, understand the nature of changing flats. If someone doesn't know how to do this at the time that they join your team, it's your job to teach them—teach them to change their own flats and to assist others who may be stranded on the road with flats. It builds character and keeps the team moving. For example, if a team member's flat is poor time management, there should be a plan in place to help him better manage his time. A reprimand alone will discourage him. With patience, you and the team can help him change his flat.

Suppose you are driving in a residential neighborhood and you encounter a series of speed bumps. They are the last thing you want to deal with. What would happen to your vehicle if you ignored them and maintained the same speed in the neighborhood as you do on the highway? The results could be devastating. Your vehicle could be severely damaged and you could receive a citation for exceeding the speed in the neighborhood. You must have the patience to go through those speed bumps and realize that the reduction in speed won't last forever. You will come again to highway that allows you to drive faster.

You must exercise the same level of patience when you drive in treacherous weather. This is not a time to increase your speed. Many accidents in severe weather conditions occur when drivers loose patience and their ability to make sound decisions becomes impaired. This is not to suggest that you have to stop driving completely when you encounter bad weather. However, you must display some degree of patience when you are thrust into a situation that is unstable and dangerous. How many leaders have we seen rush into a decision without considering all the options and the entire team suffered?

Establishing long-term success requires patience with the small things that happen to delay you temporarily. Patience is having the good-natured tolerance to get a task accomplished right the first time, so that you don't have to address the same issues over and over again. In the traffic of life, when you get a flat, don't get discouraged. You fix your flat so that you can get back on the road again.

START

Planting a flower the same time you set a goal to see which one will be completed first.

Setting a goal and sticking with it.

Using meditation.

STOP

Rushing to judgment.

Expecting instant gratification.

Giving up when the initial results are not positive.

CHAPTER TWENTY

Pot Holes

(Obstacles)

"Success is to be measured not so much by the position that one has reached in life as by the obstacles which one has overcome while trying to succeed."

Booker T. Washington

There is something you can count on every single day of your life: Something or someone will inevitably try to stop you. It's the nature of human interaction. It's not that others are evil or don't wish you well. It's not that you are a magnet for bad luck. If you live on the planet and breathe air, your daily life will be wrought with struggle. When you can say that you no longer have any struggles, you can safely say you are no longer alive.

Can you remember the last time you were driving and you encountered an obstacle in your path? Here's how one driver handled something that was blocking his path.

I live in a large city and spend about two hours a day commuting. Not a day goes by that I don't face some type of obstacle that could slow me down or completely stop me from reaching my destination. I find myself dodging stopped cars, potholes, accidents, construction, and detours.

I remember driving on the freeway and being close to the speed limit when I saw the car in front of me swerve to miss some object in its path. I only had a split second to react to the obstacle in my path. I quickly maneuvered to the right and then back to the left. I had avoided nails in the road, but just narrowly. As I drove a little further I saw several cars that had not been as fortunate. Most of those drivers ended up with flat tires. They were now dealing with two obstacles.

One of the biggest obstacles most humans face is fear. Many of us live our lives in safety nets. We avoid the things that make us most afraid. When we do so, however, we cheat ourselves out of an opportunity for improvement. We don't trust ourselves to make the right decisions during adversity and, so, we don't take the risks that would prove we have all the tools to emerge from trouble victorious. Plain and simple, fear is an obstacle and it impedes progress.

Do we shrink away from fear because we have no control over it? Do we make it larger than it needs to be? More often than not, we do. We don't like to confront the unknown. We have an insatiable need to know everything possible before we are comfortable enough to press on through uncertainty. The irony is that in our world there are a million things that we don't know at all and only a few things that we know for sure. The revolution of the world on its axis is based at least partially on the unknown. Leaders interpret uncertainty as an opportunity to actualize their leadership skills, and they move with confidence through the uncertainty, come what may.

In the traffic of life, there are obstacles that you bring on yourself, and there are obstacles that you have nothing to do with creating. Regardless of the agent that ushers these things into being, you must deal with them. Traffic accidents, death, and illness are obstacles you don't create. At times, they may seem almost insurmountable. Death, the most permanent obstacle, seems especially impossible. It is a monumental moment, a life-altering event, when everyone else gets to discover what kind of spirit dwells inside of you. No matter what you discover about yourself in this process, you are stronger for it. Anyone who has ever lost a loved one knows this.

It is possible when you are overcoming obstacles that you will not emerge without scars. Wounds are decorative in war. But in order to truly overcome something, to completely jump it and leave it behind you, you must be willing to give up your love for your wounds. Don't hang onto the thing that you are trying to defeat.

Wounds are also heavy and weigh you down. If you are a

leader and everyone sees you always weighed down, it weakens the morale of your entire team. People will begin to perceive you as the weakest member of your team and your stay in leadership will be short-lived. Even if they have assumed something about you incorrectly, remember that perception is more important at times than reality. And your team's perception could be your doom. It might also be your chance to get up again once you've been knocked down. You decide.

Dr. Melvin Gravely describes something called the "*know it when you see it principle*" in his Power of Entrepreneurial Thinking seminar. We accept things that we didn't anticipate rather than fighting our way through, or over, or around them. In some twisted way, this gives some leaders relief. They no longer have to deal with the obstacle because they have given in to it. They give themselves permission to abandon their original goals because something seems impossible. This is not ideal leadership behavior. It is accepting defeat without fighting. You always want to find a way to get over the obstacle. Even when you doubt that you can, expect wonders from yourself.

Suppose your goal is to get from your current location to see a loved one who is ill. Major construction slows you down, but are you going to let it stop you? The streets in most major cities are always under construction, so this is something you should calculate for in your daily grind. Find your way through the construction. If you fail the first time, try something different.

Sometimes your obstacle is not outside of the car, but inside. It may be your passenger. If you are traveling down the freeway at the posted speed limit trying to make it to a destination by a particular time and you have to keep stopping for your passenger to use the restroom, it is going to take you longer to reach your destination.

Through no intentional fault of their own, those passengers have become your obstacles. If you want to reach your destination, you have to find a way to do it without your passenger. In the workplace, these "passengers" thwart the productivity of the entire team. You may have to change the makeup of your team to reach your goals. You may have to change the team member's duties to things that he is more adept at doing. But something has to change–that obstacle must be overcome–if you intend to stay on course.

START

Being prepared to handle possible potholes in your path.

Understanding that troubles don't last forever.

Believing that obstacles are only speed bumps in the road of life.

Understanding you can't have a testimony without a test.

Believing you were born to excel in all aspects of your life.

STOP

Believing that bad things only happen in "your" life.

Thinking that the challenges you face are due to some form of punishment.

Believing that this obstacle will deter you from accomplishing the goals you set.

CHAPTER TWENTY-ONE

Your Sunroof

(Spirituality)

"I can do all things through Christ who strengthens me. "

Phil 4:13

Leaders do not perform the work of their lives alone. This moves beyond the work of their team members or the knowledge of mentors or educators they've had along the way. This statement speaks to the existence of a higher power. It assumes that a leader has the humility to recognize something greater than himself and honor it as an omnipotent force. Here's an account from a driver who learned to call on that humility in himself:

I remember driving out of town and getting lost because the directions I received from a friend were not that good. I was in a small town feeling lost, confused, and looking for help. Coincidentally, this was the same feeling I had at the time about my life in general. I could not believe my friend had given such bad directions or that I did not have the correct map to get me out of this situation.

I wondered what the master plan for me was and how I got so confused in my life. In my opinion, I was an excellent manager on my job and an excellent father at home. For every question anyone asked me, I thought I had all the answers. However, there was one question I didn't know the answer to. What was the next step for me?

I pulled over and parked at a rest area to gather my thoughts. The wind was blowing hard. I let all my windows down and opened my sunroof to let more of the wind come through. I remember looking up through the sunroof and seeing how clear the sky was. I wondered why the picture of my life didn't look the same. I had been facing many challenges and didn't think I could handle them all by myself.

I looked up at the heavens again and starting speaking. I asked for guidance and direction. I remember looking up and saying, "Whatever the plan is for my life, I know you won't give me more than I can bear." I knew I didn't have the answers I needed at the moment, but I had faith that if I kept looking up, the answers would be delivered to me. I had labored for weeks looking for a solution to my problems, but within one hour of peering through the sunroof, calmness, at last, entered my heart. Instantly, the answer I had been looking for came to me, and I immediately knew what direction I should be going, not only with my life but also in this small town.

A life gains clarity when you consult a higher power. In a cloudy moment—one in which a decision you need to make can determine the course of the rest of your life—you can take one of two roads: The one that leads to life eternal or the one that leads to eternal damnation. One of these paths connects you with a higher power. The other does not rely on the magic and mercy of any higher power but descends you to some dangerous depths of no return.

Both roads are bumpy and may require you to ride through storms. No journey is without turbulence. The benefit of traveling the road of life eternal, though, is that you do not travel it alone. On that path, you always have a higher power riding in the front seat with you. Cars that travel this road get a lifetime guarantee on all repairs.

If you choose the road to eternal damnation, there is only one guarantee: Your car will almost always need repair, and you will eventually run out of gas. There is one redeeming factor, however. Leaders who find themselves on the road to damnation can always make a turn onto the road of life eternal.

There will undoubtedly come a time in every person's leadership when he must call on the grace of God. A leader's ability to do so says volumes about his willingness to allow his life to be about becoming a better human every day. It is not a sign of weakness or a forfeiture to use the power of prayer to guide you through crisis or through challenging times. In fact, you might even want to adopt the practice of doing this even when everything is going well and your plans seem in perfect working order. It would be a testament that you tapped into a part of yourself that respects the natural higher hierarchy of the earth—one who is *in* authority and still respects earthly rules.

Spirituality is essential. Leaders who don't have it are merely shells and become very vulnerable at the moment they come to their first crossroads. Leaders who have strong spiritual values are happy, confident, determined, and have solid peace of mind. They usually have discovered some worship ritual that allows them to replenish themselves when they've been out tackling the sticky business of the world. Whether through traditional worship, meditation, song, or prayer, you must be administered to after you've dealt with the hard days and nights that you must face as a leader. Everyone looks to you for answers and guidance, but you must also have someone or something to look to. Not finding a way to ceremoniously attend to this need for yourself does not yield a strong base of confidence and affirmation for you as a leader. You need to know within yourself that all things are possible if you have your spiritual house in order.

In the book of Matthew in the Bible, the twelve disciples ask Christ, "Who is the greatest among us?" His answer? "The one who serves the most." He did not respond that the greatest is the one who *knows* the most. It is expected that you will not.

So the next time you are driving and you are unsure which road to take, you need only look through your sunroof and ask the heavens to show you the way. Look to your higher power and rediscover what it means to accept that you don't know the answers and be a great leader anyway.

START

Attending and participating in religious services.

Reading scriptures.

Loving your neighbor.

Praying daily.

Witnessing to others.

Giving God the praise.

STOP

Disrespecting others.

Trying to fix everything.

Thinking you are in charge.

Treating God like a spare tire and using him only when you need him.

CHAPTER TWENTY-TWO

Billboards

(Time Management)

"If you don't have the time to do it right the first time, when will you find the time to do it over?"

Anonymous

Billboards along the highway serve two purposes: 1) to sell information or products and services to consumers, and 2) to distract drivers.

How many times have you driven along the highway and seen a McDonald's billboard on the side of the road with a tempting tagline: EXIT THREE MILES. Many children find those signs completely irresistible and throw themselves into screaming fits when they see the golden arches. *Mommy, Daddy, I want to go to McDonald's!* And how could they not want to? These signs are designed to catch your attention and prompt you to act on your desires.

If drivers stopped and investigated every billboard that they saw, they would never reach their destinations. Billboards can be extremely informative, but, because they are very distracting, they also serve as roadblocks. Sometimes they can even tempt you to exit the road to find whatever they've advertised to you.

Where are the billboards in your life? Are they preventing you from achieving your daily goals? Do you manage your time well enough to invest attention in them? Or do you recognize the potential for distraction and keep on driving?

For many of us, the daily billboard that stops us dead in our tracks is the telephone, especially the friendly phone calls that do not pertain to work and cut into an already challenging day. Unfocused co-workers and friends who regularly stop by just to say hi and finagle their way into lengthy, idle discussions are also distracting billboards. The way to deal with these types of distractions is to stop them before they become habit. Make it known that your desire is not to waste time. Ask the caller or visitor if they have any work-related issues to discuss with you.

Whenever anyone says to you that he didn't get something done that he intended to do, ask how many billboards he stopped to look at that day. We con ourselves into believing that we are so busy that we have no time to accomplish the things that we say matter to us. If we led examined lives and closely scrutinized where all of our time is invested, it is almost certain that we can find time to do the things that we want to do. You must become adept at reducing or eliminating distractions and staying on course to achieve daily and long-term goals. And you must become brave enough to inform others when their intrusions deplete your availability and waste your time. If you are a leader and you seem to be struggling to meet deadlines or make it to any meeting on time, it is possible that you have too many billboards in your daily routine that you need to begin eliminating.

Sometimes distractions are planned billboards that you don't recognize as billboards. You may, for example, take a coffee break at the same time and same place every day. You may play a sporting game that continues to absorb six hours of your day, yet you never understand why you can't finish a project. Surfing the Internet for one thing can frequently turn into an all-day event.

There are tools that can help you, such as day planners, Palm Pilots, and calendars utilized by effective leaders. They have mission statements for their lives and have identified the long- and short-term goals they want to achieve. They are prepared to use their time effectively, and every second of their day counts.

Effective time management is essential to your personal growth and the growth of your team. Companies and organizations don't continue to exist without a solid understanding of the importance of managing time. There are endless billboards in a day to distract you. Your responsibility as a leader is to stay the course. Everyone is allotted only twenty-four hours a day to operate with. That time must be maximized and used efficiently. There is a saying that we will be dead longer than we are alive. If you believe that, then why waste the short time you've been given to chase billboards?

START

Using a planner or Palm Pilot to schedule your events.

On Sunday writing out your goals for the week.

Establishing ground rules with friends.

Making a calendar of your events and sending it to family and teammates.

Taping TV events that interfere with finishing your goals.

STOP

Allowing unplanned events to deter you from achieving your goals.

Procrastinating.

Ignoring Stephen Covey's habit and not "putting first things first."

CHAPTER TWENTY-THREE

Car Shopping

(Diversity)

"Never look down on anybody unless you are helping him up"

Jesse Jackson

By now, you may no longer have the old but treasured little car you had in high school. Perhaps you've purchased at least one other car and are ready for another. Even if you are not currently in the market for a new car, you may still be shopping for your dream car by browsing through the new car section of the newspaper to see what deals are being offered.

When you are ready to buy, you need to have some preset conditions before you head off to the dealership. You should have in mind what type of car you are going to purchase, what monthly payment you are willing to pay, and what the interest rate must be for you to close the deal. You should also know what options you want and what color car you have in mind. And you need to ask yourself if you are shopping for a car that will make you happy or one that you can live with that satisfies your transportation needs (the difference between the two is the amount of your payment).

Next, you should look at the service plans offered. Would you receive a loaner vehicle if you brought your car in for service? Would you get the same category loaner as the car you brought in for service? How much would you spend, on the average, for service at the dealership?

Although car dealerships have many types of vehicles, colors, models and options, they are all used for the same purpose: transportation. You may get to your destination in a Honda or Mercedes at about the same time, but not in the same style. Your choice of transportation holds a lot of promise for diversity.

When you lead a team of people, you may notice that your team members arrive with a wide variety of models, colors, options, and service plans. They will each require different levels of maintenance to keep them running efficiently. The skill you acquire at maintaining such a variety of people ensures that you can handle those who come with any combination of options. Teams with the same homogenous makeup would not give you the same opportunity to explore different solutions to problems that may be presented to you. You lose the urge to find creative options because if every person is exactly the same, then every solution to every challenge will also be the same.

It is an interesting shift in points of reference to be in Europe and see drivers on the right side of the dash inside the car and passengers on the left. It is an American tradition for drivers to operate cars in the reverse sequence. Drivers are almost always on the left. An American visiting Europe may say that Europeans drive on the *wrong*, or incorrect, side of the car. The way to view this in a way that honors and respects diversity, though, is to say that Europeans drive on the *right*, as in opposite of left, side of the car. One's respect for diversity might dictate their response upon seeing this.

You can't treat all cars the same. Each one must be responded to as an individual, diverse entity. What if you owned a luxury car and then you bought a truck to help you with heavy loads? How differently would you treat the two vehicles? As the owner, you have different expectations for each vehicle. You would not haul dirt in the luxury car nor would you drive the truck to a formal event if you did not have to. All cars have the same basic needs: cleaning, oil changes, tire rotation, preventive care, and gas to make them go. People are not much different when you deal with them in leadership. Most have some basic needs. All want to be treated with respect and be recognized when they do a job well. Most want to be developed and given an opportunity to advance.

Leaders can't always select the people who play on their team. Quite often they are forced to work with the team that is already in place. Whether you as the leader like the makeup of your team, diversity is here to stay. As demographic shifts continue to occur, diversity will become more prevalent to leaders as they guide their teams. The best leaders will learn how to make diversity an advantage over their competition.

Why is diversity so important? Think of it this way: not many people like to drive ugly cars, but they are a reality of life. Some people have a real aversion of driving next to large trucks on the freeway, but, once again, unless you stop driving you may have to drive next to a large truck because they are a reality of life. Diversity is important. People need to be able to have healthy exchanges with people who are not like themselves. Neighbors are no longer merely those who live beside you in the same neighborhood, city, state, or country. Neighbors may live in other countries. The boundaries of the Atlantic and Pacific oceans have been bridged by technology.

As a planet, we are global. If you want to compete or experience growth all over the world, you must be adept at dealing with people who don't all think, or look, or act, or feel, or live the same ways that you do. A galaxy of different ideas makes each of us a better world citizen and expands the possibilities of what we are capable of achieving.

START

Getting advice from a diverse group of people.

Taking multi-cultural classes to enhance your knowledge of cultural differences and similarities.

Accepting people for who they are and not who you want them to be.

STOP

Believing negative perceptions of other races.

Having an attitude that it's not your responsibility to create diversity in your workplace.

Believing all people should believe or act the same way.

CHAPTER TWENTY-FOUR

Rear View Mirror

(Competition)

If better is possible, good is not enough.

How many times have you been driving on the highway in the fast lane, checked your rear view mirror, and noticed someone speeding toward you? Your first instinct might have been to move over and let them pass. On the highway, this is a wise idea to avoid an accident.

In the traffic of life, that speeding car is your competition. You must be prepared to either stay in the fast lane and compete or get passed as new leaders close in on you. Before you decide that you want to get over in the slower traffic lane, make note of something: leaders should not drive in the slow lane. They should always keep up with new technology, regulations, laws, people, and industry trends to remain in the fast lane. If you see the new car coming, you are going to have to make some adjustments. If you are a top-producing salesman and have not produced in the last two quarters, but an upcoming sales representative is driving in the fast lane, you can either prepare yourself for the challenge or look in your rear view mirror and get out the way.

Competition makes you better as long as it is received in a constructive manner. By design, competition makes leaders innovative. No longer are they satisfied with doing things as they have always been done. One of the best companies to offer as proof of this is Dell Computers. In the 1990s, the battlefield for selling personal computers was highly competitive. Most computer companies were selling generic computers through retail outlets, but not Dell. All of their computers were built to order. The customer provided specifications, and the people at Dell built a computer for them. The only way to buy a Dell was by special order via the Internet or by phone order.

By using the unique model it had already developed, Dell was best positioned to capitalize on the personal computer explosion of the 1990s. For the entire decade, Dell experienced high growth and was one of the most popular companies with investors on Wall Street.

Compare Dell to Compaq and IBM, its biggest competitors during this same time period, whose use of the build-to-order model was limited. IBM chose to build computers and distribute them through retail outlets, yet Dell was able to achieve a much higher growth rate during the same period of time.

Competition makes leaders work to retain their advantage. There are an abundance of stories where we see this concept at work. An older, established leader is surpassed by the younger, innovative leader who brings new ideas to the table. Effective leaders are prepared to compete in their fields and are willing to take on new challenges.

In his "Seven Habits of Highly Effective People," Steven Covey calls this "sharpening the saw." As a leader, you must find ways to continue to develop yourself (sharpen the saw) or the competition will eventually catch up with you. How can you develop yourself? You are off to a good start by reading this book. Certainly any type of professional development training or educational classes will help you stay ahead of the competition. The key is to have a plan to stay ahead when it seems that approaching car is going to pass you by in the fast lane.

START

Understanding your competitors' strengths and weaknesses.

Keeping up with technology, laws, regulations, and people (read the newspaper daily).

Using Steven Covey's habit of "sharpening the saw." Always continue developing yourself.

STOP

Ignoring your weaknesses.

Making excuses for why the competition is better than you are.

Avoiding competition. That's how you get better.

CHAPTER TWENTY-FIVE

The Other Car

(Development)

"Many people are like a wheelbarrow they go no further than they are pushed."

Anonymous

Now that you've made it through the other twenty-four characteristics of leadership, it's time to talk about the one that should be occurring every day of your life: Development. This simply means that you continue to do whatever is necessary to realize your full potential. See how this driver helped her "new" car realize its full potential when she first got it at age sixteen:

Growing up as a teenager in Houston, Texas, had its good and bad points. One of the bad points was that you had to have a car. It did not matter if you were rich or poor. If you were a teenager even close to the age of sixteen, you needed a car. And if you didn't have one, everyone would know about it. Now, you should have begun asking and pleading for the car at age fourteen. By the time you were of legal driving age two years later, hopefully you had one.

It was now my turn to reach sixteen. I had worked hard and saved any money that I could get my hands on. I was going to buy my own car. I did not want my mother to say that I was too young to have one, or that she didn't have the money for one, or that it just was not a good idea. So, that summer I was prepared to buy my own. To my surprise, my mother had gone out and bought me a "new" old car. It was wonderful. I was now the owner of a seven-year-old, slightly used white Maverick. Yes, it was a sight for sore eyes, but to a sixteen-year-old it was a new Jaguar.

The car needed a little work before it would be ready for my friends to see it and a lot of work before it would pass inspection. With my own money, I bought new tires so that it would handle the road better and so that the wheels would not fall off while I was driving. My uncle told me everything it needed: an oil change to lubricate the metal parts to make the engine run better, gas, a new battery to store the voltage to make it start, and a little wash and wax to make it look like the gem it was.

That was the best summer of my life. With some work, that seemingly poor car turned out to be just what I needed to get me to and from work, run errands, go to parties, and do just about anything I wanted to do before 10:30 p.m.

Just as this driver did with her car, a leader helps people realize their full potential. No one attains success alone. Most companies have a personnel or human resources office responsible for training. That training can happen in several areas: computer skills, sensitivity, presentation skills, and management style. You become more efficient only by changing and developing with your company. You begin to reach for higher standards and levels of success. A company cannot grow or expand without teaching or training its employees to be successful. They must be provided with the tools and skills that they need to continue to improve their abilities to perform for the company.

Think again about that "new" old Maverick introduced to you by the driver who shared her story earlier. It was a car that she both wanted and needed; however, it was not ready to handle the task effectively. Without new tires, she was jeopardizing her safety and that of others on the highway. Without the battery and oil changes and all of the work that the car needed, it would have been a worthless heap of white metal on the side of the road, unable to perform or reach full "maverick" potential. The car needed developing. It needed more to be effective.

"People" development is essential to running any long-term successful organization. If your goal is to handle a single project and then call it quits, then there is no need to develop anyone. However, if you plan to stay in business for years to come, you must continue to develop and change with our ever-changing society and economy. Your goals will change and so must your actions.

Your customers will change and so must you. The only constant is change.

If you expect to continue to develop and maintain a level of understanding and professionalism in your industry or group, change will make a way for you and your inevitable success. You must continue to develop what you have and continue to learn.

START

Developing upcoming leaders for your position through role-playing and on-the-job training.

Providing internal and external training. Send them to leadership training and communication classes.

Having a succession plan. As current leaders leave, have future leaders already developed.

Selecting a training method of the week and utilize that week to certify everyone on the method.

STOP

Keeping all information to yourself.

Thinking that developing others will somehow diminish your position.

Ignoring the strengths and weaknesses of your group.

EPILOGUE *(TRAFFIC JAM)*

We hope that you've enjoyed **Traffic of Life** and that it has informed and inspired you as a leader. You should understand that leaders come from all walks of life and have all sorts of responsibilities. They are as *diverse* as the cars on pre-owned car lots.

One thing we have not yet mentioned is the endless *traffic jam.* There will always be traffic on the highways of your hometown and the highways of life. You know why, don't you? We are not the only drivers out there who share a dream, have a life, or simply have somewhere to go. People will always be on the roads. Here are a few things we want to make sure you remember:

If you can "start your car," you have the *desire* to get up and do something, and you've started the game.

Before you "hit the road," remember to "use a map" and set some *goals*. Driving without a plan can lead you in circles.

Sometimes it may be easier for you to **"carpool."** *Teamwork* can get you to a goal more efficiently and faster.

Accept your *flat tires.* They are just a hazard of driving, so when it happens, be *patient*.

Getting through the traffic jam is easy if you **keep gas in your car** and **service your engine** with the health and energy that will keep you in the game and ahead of the pack.

Always get **a car wash.** Your **attitude** is the key to your success.

Don't miss any *yellow lights.* If an **opportunity** comes, take it and enter the highway with **self-confidence** and determination. You can't stay on the back roads forever. One day you will have to get on the highway with the real traffic if you want to get ahead.

There are obstacles before you, but don't be afraid to take the fast lane every once in a while. Take a chance.

And when you have had all you can of that crazy traffic, take a deep breath and look through your *spiritual* sunroof. Know that you will get through the traffic eventually and appreciate it because some are still in driver's *education* learning to navigate the road.

If you ever think you have hit a road block in life, remember that you can always find a way around it by being a leader. Leadership is as easy as driving a car.

Theses are the resources that will help you flow in the Traffic of Life.

Traffic of Life Film.

This film will give you the energy to motivate your team and energize your customer base. We take everyday driving situations and turn them into leadership experiences.

Traffic of Life Game

This game creates an energetic, fun, motivating learning experience for your team or family. The game will share with you the value of using the leadership characteristics described in the book while you navigate through the obstacles of traffic. The game will teach young leaders how to lead a team and to keep driving when faced with daily potholes.

Traffic of Life Speaking Seminars

Our seminars will make you laugh out loud while motivating you through thoughtful conversation and fun role-play activities. Our speakers bring the energy that you will not soon forget.

For more information on these resources, contact us at cprseminars@aol.com

ROAD MAPS TO SUCCESS

Seven Habits of Highly Effective People
> *By Steven Covey*

Over the Top
> *By Zig Ziglar*

What Makes the Great "Great"
> *By Dennis Kimbro*

Natural Laws of Successful Time and Life Management
> *By Hyrum Smith*

Developing the Leader in You
> *By John C. Maxwell*

Becoming a Person of Influence
> *By John C. Maxwell and Jim Dornan*

Who Moved My Cheese
> *By Spencer Johnson M.D.*

Attitude is Everything
> *By Keith Harrell*

Secrets of a CEO Coach
> *By D.A. Benton*

Think and Grow Rich
> *By Napoleon Hill*

How to Win and Influence People
> *By Dale Carnegie*

The Power of E-thinking
> *By Melvin J. Gravely II*

Fish! A Remarkable Way to Boost Morale and Improve Results
> *By Stephen C. Lundin, PhD, Harry Paul and John Christensen*